Beautiful Baby Boutique II™

MW01097128

Contents

Oh, So Blue
Layette

SKILL LEVEL

EASY

FINISHED SIZES

Instructions are the same for sizes 3–6 months
and 6–12 months. Yarn, hook size and gauge
determine size. Changes for larger size are in [ ].

FINISHED MEASUREMENTS

DRESS
Chest: 22 [25] inches
Length: 11½ [13¼] inches

BLOOMERS
Waist: 22 [25] inches
Length: 7 [8] inches

BONNET
Circumference: 13½ [15½] inches
Length: 6½ [7½] inches

BOOTIES
Sole: 4½ [5¼] inches

MATERIALS

3–6 MONTHS SIZE
• Light (light worsted) weight acrylic
  yarn:
    720 yds variegated
• Size C/2/2.75mm crochet hook or size
  needed to obtain gauge
• Size D/3/3.25mm crochet hook
• 3¼ yds ¼–½-inch-wide ribbon

6–12 MONTHS SIZE
• Bernat Softee Baby light (light
  worsted) weight acrylic yarn (solids:
  5 oz/362 yds/140g; ombres: 4¼ oz/
  310 yds/120g per skein):
    3 skeins #31306 baby baby ombre

• Size D/3/3.25mm crochet hook or size
  needed to obtain gauge
• Size E/4/3.5mm crochet hook
• 5¼ yds of ¼–½-inch-wide ribbon

FOR BOTH SIZES
• Tapestry needle
• Sewing needle
• Stitch markers
• Round hook-and-loop closure
• 6 ribbon roses

GAUGE

Size C hook: 24 sc = 4 inches

Size D hook: 21 sc = 4 inches

PATTERN NOTES

Weave in ends as work progresses.

Chain-3 at beginning of row counts as double
crochet unless otherwise stated.

Join with slip stitch as indicated unless otherwise
stated.

Chain-4 at beginning of row counts as double
crochet and chain-1 unless otherwise stated.

SPECIAL STITCHES

2-double crochet shell (2-dc shell): (2 dc, ch 1,
2 dc) in indicated st or sp.

Beginning 2-double crochet shell (beg 2-dc shell):
(Ch 3, dc, ch 1, 2 dc) in indicated st or sp.

Beginning 3-double crochet shell (beg 3-dc shell):
(Ch 3, 2 dc, ch 2, 3 dc) in indicated st or sp.

3-double crochet shell (3-dc shell): (3 dc, ch 2,
3 dc) in indicated st or sp.

DRESS
YOKE

Row 1 (WS): With smaller hook, ch 67, sc in 2nd ch from hook, sc in each rem ch across, turn. *(66 sc)*

Row 2: Ch 3 *(see Pattern Notes)*, dc in each of next 9 sts, 5 dc in next st *(first corner made)*, dc in each of next 12 sts, 5 dc in next st *(2nd corner made)*, dc in each of next 18 sts, 5 dc in next st *(3rd corner made)*, dc in each of next 12 sts, 5 dc in next st *(4th corner made)*, dc in each of last 10 sts, turn. *(82 dc)*

Rows 3 & 4: Ch 3, [dc in each st to 3rd st of next corner, 5 dc in 3rd st] 4 times, dc in each rem st across, turn. *(114 dc at end of last row)*

Row 5: Ch 3, [dc in each st to 3rd st of next corner, 5 dc in 3rd st] twice, [dc in each of next 5 sts, 2 dc in next st] 4 times, dc in each of next 6 sts, 5 dc in next st, dc in each st to 3rd st of next corner, 5 dc in 3rd st, dc in each rem st across, turn. *(134 dc)*

Row 6: Ch 3, [dc in each of next 5 sts, 2 dc in next st] twice, [dc in each st to 3rd st of next corner, 5 dc in 3rd st] 4 times, [dc in each of next 5 sts, 2 dc in next st] twice, dc in each rem st across, turn. *(154 dc)*

Row 7: Ch 3, [dc in each of next 4 sts, 2 dc in next st] 3 times, dc in each st to 3rd st of next corner, 3 dc in 3rd st, dc in each of next 16 sts, 2 dc in next st, dc in each st to 3rd st of next corner, 3 dc in 3rd st, [dc in each of next 10 sts, 2 dc in next st] 3 times, dc in each st to 3rd st of next corner, 3 dc in corner st, dc in each of next 16 sts, 2 dc in next st, dc in each st to 3rd st of next corner, 3 dc in 3rd st, [dc in each of next 4 sts, 2 dc in next st] 3 times, dc in each rem st across, turn. *(173 dc)*

Row 8: With larger hook, ch 3, (dc, ch 1, 2 dc) in first st, *sk next st, **fpdc** *(see Stitch Guide)* around next dc, sk next st, **2-dc shell** *(see Special Stitches)* in next st, rep from * across, working last shell in last st, turn. *(44 shells)*

Row 9: Ch 3, 2-dc shell in first ch-1 sp, ***bpdc** *(see Stitch Guide)* around next fpdc, 2-dc shell in next ch-1 sp, rep from * across, turn.

BODY

Rnd 1 (RS): Now working in rnds, ch 3, 2-dc shell in first ch-1 sp, fpdc around next bpdc, [2-dc shell in next ch-1 sp, fpdc around next bpdc] 6 times, sk next 9 ch-1 sps, fpdc around next bpdc, [2-dc shell in next ch-1 sp, fpdc around next bpdc] 12 times, sk next 9 ch-1 sps, fpdc around next bpdc, [2-dc shell in next ch-1 sp, fpdc around next bpdc] 6 times, 2-dc shell in next ch-1 sp, **join** *(see Pattern Notes)* in 3rd ch of beg ch-3. *(26 shells)*

Rnd 2: Sl st in each st to first ch-1 sp, **beg 2-dc shell** *(see Special Stitches)* in same sp, [fpdc around next fpdc, 2-dc shell in next ch-1 sp] 6 times, fpdc around next 2 fpdc at same time, 2-dc shell in next ch-1 sp, [fpdc around next fpdc, 2-dc shell in next ch-1 sp] 11 times, fpdc around next 2 fpdc at same time, [2-dc shell in next ch-1 sp, fpdc around next fpdc] 7 times, join in 3rd ch of beg ch-3.

Rnd 3: Sl st in each st to first ch-1 sp, **beg 3-dc shell** *(see Special Stitches)* in same sp, fpdc around next fpdc, ***3-dc shell** *(see Special Stitches)* in next ch-1 sp, fpdc around next fpdc, rep from * around, join in 3rd ch of beg ch-3.

Rnds 4–16: Sl st in each st to first ch-2 sp, beg 3-dc shell in same sp, fpdc around next fpdc, *3-dc shell in next ch-2 sp, fpdc around next fpdc, rep from * around, join in 3rd ch of beg ch-3.

Rnd 17: Sl st in each st to first ch-2 sp, ch 3, 8 dc in same sp as beg ch-3, fpdc around next fpdc, *9 dc in next ch-2 sp, fpdc around next fpdc, rep from * around, join in 3rd ch of beg ch-3.

Rnd 18: Ch 1, sc in same ch as beg ch-1, *[ch 3, sk next st, sc in next st] 4 times, sk next st**, sc in next st, rep from * around, ending last rep at **, join in first sc. Fasten off.

SLEEVES

Rnd 1 (RS): With smaller hook, join yarn in first ch-1 sp to left of underarm, beg 2-dc shell in same sp, [fpdc around next bpdc, 2-dc shell in next ch-1 sp, rep from * around, fpdc around both underarm fpdc at same time, join in 3rd ch of beg ch-3. *(9 shells)*

Rnds 2–5: Sl st in each st to first ch-1 sp, beg 2-dc shell in same sp, fpdc around next fpdc, *2-dc shell in next ch-1 sp, fpdc around next fpdc, rep from * around, join in 3rd ch of beg ch-3.

Note: For longer sleeve, [rep rnd 2] 7 times.

Rnd 6: Sl st in each st to first ch-1 sp, ch 3, 6 dc in same sp as beg ch-3, fpdc around next fpdc, *7 dc in next ch-1 sp, fpdc around next fpdc, rep from * around, join in 3rd ch of beg ch-3.

Rnd 7: Ch 1, sc in same st as beg ch-1, *[ch 3, sk next st, sc in next st] 3 times, sk next st**, sc in next st, rep from * around, ending last rep at **, join in first sc. Fasten off.

Rep for rem armhole.

BACK & NECK EDGING

Rnd 1 (RS): With RS facing and smaller hook, join yarn in top right back corner, ch 1, work 16 sc down right side edge of back opening, work 16 sc up left side edge, ch 3, sk next st at neck edge, *sc in next st, ch 3, sk next st, rep from * across neck edge, join in first sc.

Row 2 (RS): Now working in rows, ch 1, sc in each sc around back opening to neck edge corner, turn.

Row 3: Ch 1, sc in each sc across. Fasten off.

FINISHING

Cut a 38 [42]-inch length of ribbon. Weave ribbon through last dc row of Yoke and tie in a bow.

Cut 2 (16 [17]-inch) lengths of ribbon. Weave one length through last shell row of each Sleeve and tie in a bow.

Sew closure to top back corners.

Sew 3 ribbon roses evenly sp across front, just above ribbon.

BLOOMERS

Rnd 1 (RS): With smaller hook, ch 96, being careful not to twist ch, **join** (*see Pattern Notes*) in first ch to form ring, ch 1, sc in each ch around, join in first sc. (*96 sc*)

Rnd 2: Ch 1, sc in each sc around, join in first sc.

Rnd 3: **Beg 2-dc shell** (*see Special Stitches*) in same st as joining, sk next st, dc in next st, *sk next st, **2-dc shell** (*see Special Stitches*) in next st, sk next st, dc in next st, rep from * around, join in 3rd ch of beg ch-3. (*24 shells*)

Rnds 4: Sl st in each st to first ch-1 sp, beg 2-dc shell in same sp, **fpdc** (*see Stitch Guide*) around next dc, *2-dc shell in next ch-1 sp, fpdc around next dc, rep from * around, join in 3rd ch of beg ch-3.

Rnds 5–18: Sl st in each st to first ch-1 sp, beg 2-dc shell in same sp, fpdc around next fpdc, *2-dc shell in next ch-1 sp, fpdc around next fpdc, rep from * around, join in 3rd ch of beg ch-3.

CROTCH PANEL

Row 1: Now working in rows, ch 1, sc in same st as beg ch-1, sc in each of next 4 sts of shell, [sc in next fpdc, sc in each of next 5 sts of next shell] twice, turn. (*17 sc*)

Rows 2–13: Ch 1, sc in each sc across, turn. At end of last row, leaving a long tail, fasten off.

ASSEMBLY

Using tapestry needle and yarn tail, sew Crotch Panel to other side of Bloomers, leaving 9 shells unworked on either side for leg openings.

LEG EDGING

Rnd 1 (RS): Join yarn with a sc in first unworked fpdc at leg opening, [2 sc in next ch-1 sp, sc in next fpdc] 9 times, work 6 sc down side edge of Crotch Panel, join in first sc. (*34 sc*)

Rnds 2 & 3: Ch 1, sc in each sc around, join in first sc.

Rnd 4: Ch 1, sc in same st as beg ch-1, [ch 4, sk next st, sc in next st] 16 times, ch 1, join with dc in first sc. (*17 ch sps*)

Rnd 5: Ch 1, sc in sp formed by joining dc, ch 4, [sc in next ch-4 sp, ch 4] 16 times, join in first sc. Fasten off.

Work Leg Edging around 2nd leg opening in same manner.

FINISHING

Cut a 38 [42]-inch length of ribbon. Weave ribbon through topmost shell rnd and tie in a bow.

BONNET

Rnd 1 (RS): With smaller hook, ch 6, **join** (*see Pattern Notes*) in first ch to form ring, **ch 3** (*see Pattern Notes*), 15 dc in ring, join in 3rd ch of beg ch-3. (*16 dc*)

Rnds 2–4: Ch 3, 2 dc in next st, *dc in next st, 2 dc in next st, rep from * around, join in 3rd ch of beg ch-3. (*54 dc at end of last rnd*)

Rnd 5: Ch 3, dc in next dc, 2 dc in next dc, *dc in each of next 2 dc, 2 dc in next dc, rep from * around, join in 3rd ch of beg ch-3. (*72 dc*)

Row 6 (RS): Now working in rows, ch 3, [**fpdc** (*see Stitch Guide*) around next dc, sk next st, **2-dc shell** (*see Special Stitches*) in next st, sk next st] 14 times, fpdc around next dc, dc in next st, leaving rem sts unworked, turn.

Row 7: Ch 3, [**bpdc** (*see Stitch Guide*) around next fpdc, 2-dc shell in next ch-1 sp] 14 times, bpdc around next fpdc, dc in last st, turn.

Row 8: Ch 3, [fpdc around next bpdc, 2-dc shell in next ch-1 sp] 14 times, fpdc around next bpdc, dc in last st, turn.

Rows 9–14: [Rep rows 7 and 8 alternately] 3 times.

Row 15: Rep row 7.

Row 16: Ch 3, 7 dc in next ch-1 sp, [fpdc around next bpdc, 7 dc in next ch-1 sp] 14 times, dc in last st. **Do not turn.**

EDGING
Rnd 1 (RS): Work 16 sc evenly sp across next side of Bonnet, work 8 sc evenly sp across back neck edge, work 16 sc evenly sp across next side of Bonnet, sc in first dc of 7-dc group at front edge, *[ch 3, sk next st, sc in next st] 3 times**, sk next st, sc in next st, rep from * around, ending last rep at **, join in first sc.

Row 2 (RS): Now working in rows, ch 1, sc in same sc as beg ch-1, sc in each of next 40 sc, turn.

Row 3: Ch 1, sc in each sc across. Fasten off.

FINISHING
Cut a 28 [30]-inch length of ribbon. Weave ribbon through sps on row 11 for ties.

Sew a ribbon rose to center of row 15 of Bonnet.

BOOTIE
MAKE 2.
CUFF
Rnd 1 (RS): With smaller hook, ch 30, being careful not to twist ch, **join** *(see Pattern Notes)* in first ch to form ring, **ch 4** *(see Pattern Notes)*, sk next ch, *dc in next ch, ch 1, sk next ch, rep from * around, join in 3rd of beg ch-4. *(15 ch sps)* Mark center 3 sps.

Rnd 2: Sl st in next ch sp, **beg 3-dc shell** *(see Special Stitches)* in same sp, sk next ch sp, **fpdc** *(see Stitch Guide)* around next dc, [sk next ch sp, **3-dc shell** *(see Special Stitches)* in next ch sp, sk next ch sp, fpdc around next dc] 4 times, join in 3rd ch of beg ch-3. *(5 shells)*

Rnds 3 & 4: Sl st in each st to next ch-2 sp, beg 3-dc shell in same sp, fpdc around next fpdc, *3-dc shell in next ch-2 sp, fpdc around next fpdc, rep from * around, join in 3rd ch of beg ch-3.

Rnd 5: Sl st in each st to next ch-1 sp, **ch 3** *(see Pattern Notes)*, 6 dc in same sp as beg ch-3, fpdc around next fpdc, *7 dc in next ch-1 sp, fpdc around next fpdc, rep from * around, join in 3rd ch of beg ch-3.

Rnd 6: Ch 1, sc in same st as beg ch-1, *[ch 3, sk next st, sc in next st] 3 times, sk next st**, sc in next st, rep from * around, ending last rep at **, join in first sc. Fasten off.

INSTEP
Row 1 (RS): With RS facing, holding Cuff upside down and with smaller hook, join yarn with sc in first marked sp, 2 sc in same sp, 3 sc in each of next 2 sps, turn. *(9 sc)*

Rows 2–6: Ch 1, sc in each sc across, turn. At end of last row, fasten off.

FOOT & SOLE
Row 1 (RS): With RS facing, holding Cuff upside down and with smaller hook, join yarn in joining sl st of beg ch-30 ring, ch 3, 2 dc in each of next 6 sps, work 6 dc across side edge of Instep, work 9 dc across top of Instep, work 6 dc across side edge of Instep, 2 dc in each of next 6 sps on Cuff, join in 3rd ch of beg ch-3. *(46 dc)*

Rnds 2 & 3: Now working in rnds, ch 3, dc in each st around, join in 3rd ch of beg ch-3.

Rnd 4: Ch 3, **dc dec** *(see Stitch Guide)* in next 3 sts, dc in each of next 15 sts, [dc dec in next 3 sts] 3 times, dc in each of next 15 sts, dc dec in next 3 sts, join in 3rd ch of beg ch 3. Leaving 12-inch tail, fasten off. *(36 dc)*

FINISHING
Turn Booties inside out. With tapestry needle and long tail, sew opening closed.

Cut 2 (16 [17]-inch) lengths of ribbon. Weave ribbon through row 1 of each Cuff and tie in a bow.

Sew 1 ribbon rose to each Instep. ■

Gumdrop *Layette*

SKILL LEVEL

EASY

FINISHED SIZE
6–12 months

FINISHED MEASUREMENTS

SWEATER
Chest: 25½ inches
Length: 9½ inches

BONNET
Circumference: 14 inches
Length: 7 inches

BOOTIES
Sole: 4¾ inches

MATERIALS
- Fine (sport) weight acrylic yarn: 460 yds green/yellow/blue variegated 100 yds white
- Size E/4/3.5mm crochet hook or size needed to obtain gauge
- Tapestry needle
- Sewing needle
- Stitch marker
- 3¼ yds of ¼–½-inch-wide ribbon
- ½-inch decorative buttons: 2
- Matching sewing thread

GAUGE
20 dc = 4 inches; 4 shells = 4 inches

PATTERN NOTES
Weave in ends as work progresses.

Chain-3 at beginning of row counts as double crochet unless otherwise stated.

Join with slip stitch as indicated unless otherwise stated.

Chain-4 at beginning of round counts as double crochet and chain-1 unless otherwise stated.

SPECIAL STITCHES
Shell: (**Puff st**—*see Special Stitches*, ch 2, puff st, ch 1) in indicated st.

Puff stitch (puff st): [Yo, pull up lp in indicated st and pull it out to about ½ inch tall] 3 times, yo and draw through all 7 lps on hook.

Beginning shell (beg shell): (**Beg puff st**—*see Special Stitches*, ch 2, puff st, ch 1) in indicated st.

Beginning puff stitch (beg puff st): Ch 3, [yo, pull up lp in indicated st and pull it out to about ½ inch tall] twice, yo and draw though all 5 lps on hook.

SWEATER
YOKE
Row 1 (WS): With variegated, ch 70, sc in 2nd ch from hook, sc in each rem ch across, turn. *(69 sc)*

Row 2: Ch 3 *(see Pattern Notes)*, dc in each st across, inc 11 dc evenly sp, turn. *(80 dc)*

Row 3: Ch 1, sc in each st across, inc 11 sc evenly sp, turn. *(91 sc)*

Rows 4 & 5: Rep rows 2 and 3. *(113 sc)*

Row 6: Ch 3, dc in each st across, inc 10 dc evenly sp, turn. *(123 dc)*

Row 7: Ch 1, sc in each st across, turn. *(123 sc)*

Row 8: Ch 3, dc in next st, *sk next 2 sts, **shell** (*see Special Stitches*) in next st, rep from * across to last 4 sts, sk next 2 sts, dc in each of last 2 sts, turn. (*39 shells*)

Rows 9–11: Ch 3, dc in next dc, shell in each ch-2 sp across, dc in each of last 2 sts, turn.

BODY

Row 1 (RS): Ch 3, dc in next dc, shell in each of next 6 ch-2 sps, sk next 7 ch-2 sps, shell in each of next 13 ch-2 sps, sk next 7 ch-2 sps, shell in each of next 6 ch-2 sps, dc in each of last 2 sts, turn. (*25 shells*)

Rows 2–8: Ch 3, dc in next dc, shell in each ch-2 sp across, dc in each of last 2 sts, turn. **Change color** (*see Stitch Guide*) to white in last st of row 8.

EDGING

Rnd 1 (RS): Ch 3, dc in next dc, *ch 1, ([puff st, ch 2] twice, puff st) in next ch-2 sp, ch 1, sc in next ch-1 sp, rep from * across to last ch-2 sp, ch 1, ([puff st, ch 2] twice, puff st) in next ch-2 sp, ch 1, dc in each of last 2 sts, **ch 3, sc in top of edge st, rep from ** up right front edge, ch 3, sc in top right front corner, ***ch 3, sk next st, sc in next st, rep from *** across neck edge, [ch 3, sc in top of edge st] down left front neck edge, ch 3, join in 3rd of beg ch-3. Fasten off.

SLEEVE

Rnd 1 (RS): With RS facing, join variegated at underarm sp, **beg shell** (*see Special Stitches*) in same sp as beg ch-3, shell in each of sk 7 ch-2 sps, join in beg shell. (*8 shells*)

Rnds 2–9: Sl st in next ch-2 sp, beg shell in same sp, shell in each of next 7 ch-2 sps, join in beg shell.

Rnd 10: Sl st in next ch-2 sp, ch 1, 3 sc in same sp as beg ch-1, 3 sc in each rem ch-2 sp around, join in first sc. (*24 sc*)

Rnd 11: Ch 1, sc in each st around, join in first sc. Change to B at end of rnd.

Rnd 12: *Ch 3, sk next st, sc in next st, rep from * around, join in base of beg ch-3. Fasten off.

FINISHING

Cut a 30-inch length of ribbon. Weave ribbon through topmost dc row and tie in a bow.

Cut 2 (9-inch) lengths of ribbon. Sew 1 end of each ribbon to each edge of topmost shell row. Sew decorative button on top of each sewn end. Tie ends in bows.

BONNET

Rnd 1 (RS): With variegated, ch 7, **join** (*see Pattern Notes*) in first ch to form ring, **ch 3** (*see Pattern Notes*), 23 dc in ring, join in 3rd ch of beg ch-3. (*24 dc*)

Rnd 2: Ch 3, dc in next dc, 2 dc in next dc, *dc in each of next 2 dc, 2 dc in next dc, rep from * around, join in 3rd ch of beg ch-3. (*32 dc*)

Rnd 3: Ch 3, dc in next dc, *2 dc in next dc, dc in each of next 2 dc, rep from * around, join in 3rd ch of beg ch-3. (*42 dc*)

Rnd 4: Rep rnd 2. (*56 dc*)

BODY

Row 1 (RS): Now working in rows, ch 3, dc in next st, [sk next 2 sts, **shell** (*see Special Stitches*) in next st] 13 times, sk next 2 sts, dc in each of next 2 sts, leave rem sts unworked, turn. (*13 shells*)

Row 2–8: Ch 3, dc in next dc, shell in each ch-2 sp across, dc in each of last 2 sts. **Change color** (*see Stitch Guide*) to white in last st of row 8.

EDGING

Rnd 1 (RS): Ch 1, sc in first st, *ch 1, ([puff st, ch 2] twice, puff st) in next ch-2 sp, ch 1, sc in next ch-1 sp, rep from * to end, sc in last st, working across edge of Body, work 16 sc evenly sp across, working across back neck edge, work 8 sc evenly sp across, working across next edge of Body, work 16 sc across, join in first sc, turn.

Row 2 (WS): Ch 1, sc in each of first 40 sc. Leaving rem sts unworked, fasten off.

FINISHING

Cut a 28-inch length of ribbon. Weave ribbon through bottom shell row of Bonnet for ties.

BOOTIE
MAKE 2.
SOLE & FOOT

Rnd 1 (RS): Ch 12, 3 sc in 2nd ch from hook, sc in each of next 9 chs, 3 sc in last ch, working in unused lps on opposite side of foundation ch, sc in each of next 9 chs, **join** *(see Pattern Notes)* in first sc. *(24 sc)*

Rnd 2: Ch 1, 2 sc in first sc, 2 sc in each of next 3 sts, sc in each of next 8 sts, 2 sc in each of next 4 sts, sc in each of next 8 sts, join in first sc. *(32 sc)*

Rnd 3: Ch 1, sc in first sc, [2 sc in next sc, sc in next sc] 4 times, sc in each of next 8 sc, [2 sc in next sc, sc in next sc] 4 times, sc in each of next 7 sc, join in first sc. *(40 sc)*

Rnds 4–6: Ch 1, sc in each sc around, join in first sc. At end of last rnd, fasten off.

INSTEP

Note: Fold sole in half lengthwise and mark 1 of end sts as center back st.

Row 1 (RS): With RS facing, count 16 sts away from marked st, join variegated with a sc in next st, sc in each of next 7 sts, sl st in next st on side of foot, turn.

Rnds 2–9: Ch 1, sc in each of first 8 sc, sl st in next st on side of foot, turn. At end of last row, fasten off.

CUFF

Rnd 1 (RS): With RS facing, join variegated at marked center back st, ch 1, sc in same st as beg ch-1, sc in each of next 12 sts at side of foot, sc in each of next 3 sc on instep, **sc dec** *(see Stitch Guide)* in next 2 sc, sc in each of next 3 sc, sc in each of next 12 sts at other side of foot, join in first sc. *(32 sc)*

Rnd 2: **Ch 3** *(see Pattern Notes)*, dc in each st around, join in 3rd ch of beg ch-3.

Rnd 3: **Beg shell** *(see Special Stitches)* in same st as beg ch-3, sk next 3 sts, *shell *(see Special Stitches)* in next st, sk next 3 sts, rep from * around, join in beg shell. *(8 shells)*

Rnd 4: Sl st in next ch-2 sp, beg shell in same sp, shell in each of next 7 ch-2 sps, join in beg shell. Fasten off.

Rnd 5: With RS facing, join white in any ch-1 sp, ch 1, sc in same sp as beg ch-1, *ch 1, ([puff st, ch 2] twice, puff st) in next ch-2 sp, ch 1, sc in next ch-1 sp, rep from * across to last ch-2 sp, ch 1, ([puff st, ch 2] twice, puff st) in last ch-2 sp, ch 1, join in first sc. Fasten off.

FINISHING

Cut 2 (18-inch) lengths of ribbon. Weave ribbon through row 2 of each Cuff and tie in a bow. ∎

Sweet Pea
Layette

SKILL LEVEL

EASY

FINISHED SIZES
Instructions are the same for sizes 0–3 months and 6–12 months. Yarn, hook size and gauge determine size. Changes for larger size are in [ ].

FINISHED MEASUREMENTS
SWEATER
Chest: 18½ [21¾] inches
Length: 8½ [9¾] inches

BONNET
Circumference: 13 [14¾] inches
Length: 5¾ [6½] inches with brim folded up

BOOTIES
Sole: 4½ [5¼] inches

MATERIALS
0–3 MONTHS SIZE
- Red Heart Baby TLC acrylic yarn (5 oz/358 yds/151g per skein): 2 skeins #5737 powder pink
- Size C/2/2.75mm crochet hook or size needed to obtain gauge
- Size D/3/3.25mm crochet hook
- Tapestry needle
- 2¾ yds ¼–½-inch ribbon

6–12 MONTHS SIZE
- Bernat Softee Baby light (light worsted) weight acrylic yarn (5 oz/362 yds/140g per skein): 2 skeins #02001 pink
- Size D/3/3.25mm crochet hook or size needed to obtain gauge
- Size E/3/3.5mm crochet hook

- Tapestry needle
- 2¾ yds ¼–½-inch ribbon

FOR BOTH SIZES
- Tapestry needle
- Stitch markers

GAUGE
Size C hook: 24 sc = 4 inches

Size D hook: 21 sc = 4 inches

PATTERN NOTES
Weave in ends as work progresses.

Chain-3 at beginning of row counts as double crochet unless otherwise stated.

Join with slip stitch as indicated unless otherwise stated.

SPECIAL STITCHES
2-double crochet shell (2-dc shell): (2 dc, ch 2, 2 dc) in indicated st or sp.

3-double crochet shell (3-dc shell): (3 dc, ch 2, 3 dc) in indicated st or sp.

Beginning 2-double crochet shell (beg 2-dc shell): (Ch 3, dc, ch 2, 2 dc) in indicated st or sp.

SWEATER
YOKE
Row 1 (RS): With smaller hook, ch 62, sc in 2nd ch from hook, sc in each rem ch across, turn. (*61 sc*)

Row 2: Ch 3 (*see Pattern Notes*), dc in each st across, turn. (*61 dc*)

Rows 3–6: Ch 3, dc in each st, inc 20 evenly sp across, turn. (*141 sts at end of last row*)

Row 7: With larger hook, ch 3, *sk next 2 sts, **2-dc shell** (see Special Stitches) in next sp between sts, sk next 2 sts, **fpdc** (see Stitch Guide) around next st, rep from * across to last 5 sts, sk next 2 sts, 2-dc shell in next sp between sts, sk next 2 sts, dc in last st, turn. (28 2-dc shells)

Row 8: Ch 3, *2-dc shell in next ch-2 sp, **bpdc** (see Stitch Guide) around next fpdc, rep from * across to last ch-2 sp, 2-dc shell in last ch-2 sp, dc in last st, turn.

Row 9: Ch 3, *2-dc shell in next ch-2 sp, fpdc around next bpdc, rep from * across to last ch-2 sp, 2-dc shell in last ch-2 sp, dc in last st, turn.

BODY

Row 1 (WS): Ch 3, [2-dc shell in next ch-2 sp, bpdc around next fpdc] 4 times, sk next 6 shells, bpdc around next fpdc, [2-dc shell in next ch-2 sp, bpdc around next fpdc] 8 times, sk next 6 shells, bpdc around next fpdc, [2-dc shell in next ch-2 sp, bpdc around next fpdc] 3 times, 2-dc shell in next ch-2 sp, dc in last st, turn. (16 shells)

Row 2 (RS): Ch 3, [2-dc shell in next ch-2 sp, fpdc around next bpdc] 3 times, 2-dc shell in next ch-2 sp, fpdc around next 2 bpdc at the same time, [2-dc shell in next ch-2 sp, fpdc around next bpdc] 7 times, 2-dc shell in next ch-2 sp, fpdc around next 2 bpdc at the same time, [2-dc shell in next ch-2 sp, fpdc around next bpdc] 3 times, 2-dc shell in next ch-2 sp, dc in last st, turn.

Row 3: Ch 3, *2-dc shell in next ch-2 sp, bpdc around next fpdc, rep from * across to last ch-2 sp, 2-dc shell in last ch-2 sp, dc in last st, turn.

Row 4: Ch 3, *2-dc shell in next ch-2 sp, fpdc around next bpdc, rep from * across to last ch-2 sp, 2-dc shell in last ch-2 sp, dc in last st, turn.

Row 5: Rep row 3.

Row 6: Ch 3, *3-dc shell (see Special Stitches) in next ch-2 sp, fpdc around next bpdc, rep from * across to last ch-2 sp, 3-dc shell in last ch-2 sp, dc in last st, turn.

Row 7: Ch 3, *3-dc shell in next ch-2 sp, bpdc around next fpdc, rep from * across to last ch-2 sp, 3-dc shell in last ch-2 sp, dc in last st, turn.

Rows 8–11: [Rep rows 6 and 7 alternately] twice.

Row 12: Ch 3, *7 dc in next ch-2 sp, fpdc around next bpdc, rep from * across to last ch-2 sp, 7 dc in last ch-2 sp, dc in last st. Fasten off.

SLEEVES

Rnd 1 (RS): With RS facing and larger hook, join yarn at center underarm dc, **beg 2-dc shell** (see Special Stitches) in same st as joining, fpdc around next fpdc, [2-dc shell in next unworked ch-2 sp on Sleeve, fpdc around next fpdc] 6 times, join in 3rd ch of beg ch-3 of beg 2-dc shell.

Rnds 2–10: Sl st in next st and in next ch-2 sp, beg 2-dc shell in same ch-2 sp, fpdc around next fpdc, [2-dc shell in ch-2 sp of next 2-dc shell, fpdc around next fpdc] 6 times, join in beg 2-dc shell.

Rnd 11: Sl st in next st and in next ch-2 sp, ch 3, 4 dc in same sp, [fpdc around next fpdc, 5 dc in next ch-2 sp] 6 times, fpdc around next fpdc, join in 3rd ch of beg ch-3. Fasten off.

Rep in rem armhole.

FINISHING

Cut a 28 [30]-inch length of ribbon. Weave ribbon through topmost dc row of yoke and tie in a bow.

BONNET

Rnd 1 (RS): With smaller hook, ch 7, **join** (see Pattern Notes) in first ch to form ring, **ch 3** (see Pattern Notes), 23 dc in ring, join in 3rd ch of beg ch-3. (24 dc)

Rnd 2: Ch 3, 2 dc in next st, *dc in next st, 2 dc in next st, rep from * around, join in 3rd ch of beg ch-3. (36 dc)

Rnd 3: Ch 3, dc in next st, 2 dc in next st, *dc in each of next 2 sts, 2 dc in next st, rep from * around, join in 3rd ch of beg ch-3. (48 dc)

BODY

Row 1 (RS): Now working in rows, ch 3, **fpdc** *(see Stitch Guide)* around next st, [sk 2 sts, **3-dc shell** *(see Special Stitches)* in next sp between sts, sk next 2 sts, fpdc around next st] 7 times, dc in next dc, leaving rem sts unworked, turn. *(7 shells)*

Row 2: Ch 3, **bpdc** *(see Stitch Guide)* around next fpdc, *3-dc shell in next ch-2 sp, bpdc around next fpdc, rep from * across to last st, dc in last st, turn.

Row 3: Ch 3, fpdc around next bpdc, *3-dc shell in next ch-2 sp, fpdc around next bpdc, rep from * across to last st, dc in last st, turn.

Rows 4–11: [Rep rows 2 and 3 alternately] 4 times.

Row 12: Ch 3, bpdc around next fpdc, *5 dc in next ch-2 sp, bpdc around next fpdc, rep from * across to last st, dc in last st. Do not turn.

EDGING

Row 1 (WS): Ch 1, working across side of Body, work 17 sc evenly sp across edge, working across back neck edge, work 9 sc evenly sp across edge, working across next edge of Body, work 16 sc evenly sp across edge, turn. *(42 sc)*

Rows 2 & 3: Ch 1, sc in each sc across, turn.

Row 4: **Ch 4** *(see Pattern Notes)*, sk next st, dc in next st, *ch 1, sk next st, dc in next st, rep from * across. Fasten off. *(22 dc)*

FINISHING

Fold up top 2 rows of Bonnet and tack down.

Cut a 26 [28]-inch length of ribbon. Weave ribbon through last row of Bonnet Edging for ties.

BOOTIE
MAKE 2.
CUFF

Rnd 1 (RS): Using smaller hook, ch 30, being careful not to twist ch, **join** *(see Pattern Notes)* in first ch to form ring, **ch 4** *(see Pattern Notes)*, sk next ch, *dc in next ch, ch 1, sk next ch, rep from * around, join in 3rd ch of beg ch-4. Mark center 3 sps. *(15 ch-1 sps)*

Rnd 2: **Ch 3** *(see Pattern Notes)*, sk next sp, **3-dc shell** *(see Special Stitches)* in next ch-1 sp, sk next ch-1 sp, [**fpdc** *(see Stitch Guide)* around next st, sk next ch-1 sp, 3-dc shell in next ch-1 sp, sk next ch-1 sp] 4 times, join in 3rd ch of beg ch-3. *(5 shells)*

Rnds 3 & 4: Ch 3, 3-dc shell in next ch-2 sp, [fpdc around next fpdc, 3-dc shell in next ch-2 sp] 4 times, join in 3rd ch of beg ch-3.

Rnd 5: Ch 3, 7 dc in next ch-2 sp, [fpdc around next fpdc, 7 dc in next ch-2 sp] 4 times, join in 3rd ch of beg ch-3. Fasten off.

INSTEP

Row 1 (RS): With RS facing, holding cuff upside down and with smaller hook, join yarn with sc in first marked sp, 2 sc in same sp, 3 sc in each of next 2 sps, turn. *(9 sc)*

Rows 2–6: Ch 1, sc in each sc across. At end of last row, fasten off.

FOOT & SOLE

Row 1 (RS): With RS facing, holding cuff upside down and with smaller hook, join yarn in joining sl st of foundation ring, ch 3, 2 dc in each of next 6 sps, work 6 dc evenly sp along side edge of Instep, work 9 dc evenly sp across top of Instep, work 6 dc evenly sp along side edge of Instep, 2 dc in each of next 6 sps on Cuff, join in 3rd ch of beg ch-3. *(46 dc)*

Rnds 2 & 3: Ch 3, dc in each st around, join in 3rd ch of beg ch-3.

Rnd 4: Ch 3, **dc dec** *(see Stitch Guide)* in next 3 sts, dc in each of next 15 sts, [dc dec in next 3 sts] 3 times, dc in each of next 15 sts, dc dec in next 3 sts, join in 3rd ch of beg ch-3. Leaving 12-inch tail, fasten off. *(36 dc)*

FINISHING

Turn Booties inside out. With tapestry needle and long tails, sew openings closed.

Cut 2 (16 [17]-inch) lengths of ribbon. Weave ribbon through row 1 of each Cuff and tie in a bow. ∎

Molly Shell & Pineapple
Dress & Hat

SKILL LEVEL

EASY

FINISHED SIZES

Instructions are same for sizes 6 months and 12 months. Hook size and gauge determine size. Changes for larger size are in [ ].

FINISHED MEASUREMENTS

DRESS
Chest: 20 [21¾] inches
Length: 14 [15¼] inches

HAT
Circumference: 18 [19½] inches
Length: 7 [7¾] inches

BOOTIES
Sole: 4¾ [5¼] inches

MATERIALS

- Bernat Baby super fine (fingering) weight acrylic/nylon yarn (1¾ oz/ 191 yds/50g per skein): 3 [4] skeins #35436 yellow
- Size C/2/2.75mm [D/3/3.25mm] crochet hook or size needed to obtain gauge
- Tapestry needle
- Sewing needle
- 2¼ [2½] yds ¼–½-inch-wide ribbon
- 2 ribbon roses (optional)
- 3 snaps
- Matching sewing thread

GAUGE

Size C hook: 6 shells = 4 inches; 10 rows = 4 inches

Size D hook: 5½ shells = 4 inches; 9 rows = 4 inches

PATTERN NOTES

Weave in ends as work progresses.

Chain-3 at beginning of row or round counts as double crochet unless otherwise stated.

Join with slip stitch as indicated unless otherwise stated.

Chain-4 at beginning of round counts as double crochet and chain-1 unless otherwise stated.

SPECIAL STITCHES

Shell: (2 dc, ch 1, 2 dc) in indicated st or sp.

Corner shell: ([2 dc, ch 1] twice, 2 dc) in indicated st or sp.

Chain-2 shell (ch-2 shell): (2 dc, ch 2, 2 dc) in indicated st or sp.

Beginning chain-2 shell (beg ch-2 shell): (Ch 3, dc, ch 2, 2 dc) in indicated st or sp.

V-stitch (V-st): Dc, ch 4, dc) in indicated st or sp.

3-double crochet cluster (3-dc cl): Holding back last lp of each dc on hook, 3 dc in indicated st or sp, yo and draw through all 4 lps on hook.

Picot: Ch 4, sc at base of ch-4.

DRESS
BODICE

Row 1 (RS): Ch 74, sc in 2nd ch from hook, sc in each rem ch across, turn. *(73 sc)*

Row 2: Ch 1, sc in first sc, sc in next sc, *2 sc in next sc, sc in each of next 2 sc, rep from * across to last 2 sts, 2 sc in next sc, sc in last sc, turn. *(97 sc)*

Row 3: Ch 3 (see Pattern Notes), dc in each of next 2 sts, sk next 3 sts, *shell (see Special Stitches) in next st, sk next 3 sts, rep from * across to last 7 sts, shell in next st, sk next 3 sts, dc in each of last 3 sts, turn. (22 shells)

Row 4: Ch 3, dc in each of next 2 sts, [shell in ch-1 sp of each of next 3 shells, **corner shell** (see Special Stitches) in ch-1 sp of next shell] twice, shell in ch-1 sp of each of next 6 shells, [corner shell in ch-1 sp of next shell, shell in ch-1 sp of each of next 3 shells] twice, dc in each of last 3 sts, turn. (18 shells, 4 corner shells)

Row 5: Ch 3, dc in each of next 2 sts, shell each ch-1 sp across, dc in each of last 3 sts, turn. (26 shells)

Row 6: Ch 3, dc in each of next 2 sts, shell in each of next 4 shells, corner shell in next sp between shells, shell in each of next 5 shells, corner shell in next sp between shells, shell in each of next 8 shells, corner shell in next sp between shells, shell in each of next 5 shells, corner shell in next sp between shells, shell in each of next 4 shells, dc in each of last 3 sts, turn. (26 shells, 4 corner shells)

Row 7: Rep row 5. (34 shells)

Row 8: Ch 3, dc in each of next 2 sts, shell in each of next 5 shells, corner shell in next sp between shells, shell in each of next 7 shells, corner shell in next sp between shells, shell in each of next 10 shells, corner shell in next sp between shells, shell in each of next 7 shells, corner shell in next sp between shells, shell in each of next 5 shells, dc in each of last 3 sts, turn. (34 shells, 4 corner shells)

Row 9: Ch 3, dc in each of next 2 sts, shell each of next 6 ch-1 sps, ch 2 (corner sp made), shell in each of next 9 ch -1 sps, ch 2 (corner sp made), shell in each of next 12 ch-1 sps, ch 2 (corner sp made), shell in each of next 9 ch-1 sps, ch 2 (corner sp made), shell in each of next 6 ch-1 sps, dc in each of last 3 sts, turn. (42 shells)

BODY

Row 1 (WS): Ch 3, dc in each of next 2 sts, **ch-2 shell** (see Special Stitches) in each of next 6 shells, ch-2 shell in next ch-2 sp, ch 5 (underarm made), sk next 9 shells, ch-2 shell in next ch-2 sp, ch-2 shell in each of next 12 shells, ch-2 shell in next ch-2 sp, ch 5 (underarm made), sk next 9 shells, ch-2 shell in next ch-2 sp, ch-2 shell in each of next 6 shells, dc in each of last 3 sts, turn. (28 shells)

Row 2: Ch 3, dc in each of next 2 sts, ch-2 shell in each of next 7 shells, ch-2 shell in 3rd ch of next ch-5, shell in each of next 14 shells, ch-2 shell in 3rd ch of next ch-5, ch-2 shell in each of next 7 shells, dc in each of last 3 sts, turn. (30 ch-2 shells)

Row 3: Ch 3, dc in each of next 2 sts, ch-2 shell in next shell, *ch 1, (2 dc, ch 4, 2 dc) in next shell, ch 1, ch-2 shell in next shell, ch 1, dc in next sp between shells, ch 1, ch-2 shell in next shell, rep from * across to last 2 shells, ch 1, (2 dc, ch 4, 2 dc) in next shell, ch 1, ch-2 shell in last shell, dc in each of last 3 sts, turn. (20 ch-2 shells, 10 ch-4 sps)

Row 4: Ch 3, dc in each of next 2 sts, ch-2 shell in next shell, *ch 1, 7 dc in next ch-4 sp, ch 1, ch-2 shell in next shell, ch 1, sk next 2 dc of shell, dc in next dc, ch 1, ch-2 shell in next shell, rep from * across to last ch-4 sp, ch 1, 7 dc in last ch-4 sp, ch 1, ch-2 shell in last shell, dc in each of last 3 sts, turn.

Row 5: Ch 3, dc in each of next 2 sts, ch-2 shell in next shell, *ch 2, sk next 2 dc of shell, dc in first dc of next 7-dc group, [ch 1, dc in next dc] 6 times, ch 2, ch-2 shell in next shell, ch 1, sk next 2 dc of shell, dc in next dc, ch 1, ch-2 shell in next shell, rep from * across to last 7-dc group, ch 2, sk next 2 dc of shell, dc in first dc of next 7-dc group, [ch 1, dc in next dc] 6 times, ch 2, ch-2 shell in last shell, dc in each of last 3 sts, turn.

Rnd 1 (RS): Now working in rnds, ch 2, **dc dec** (see Stitch Guide) in next 2 sts, *ch-2 shell in next shell, ch 2, sk next 2 dc of shell, sc in next dc, [ch 4, sc in next dc] 6 times, ch 2, ch-2 shell in next shell**, ch 1, sk next 2 dc of shell, dc in next dc, ch 1, rep from * around, ending last rep at **, dc dec in last 3 sts, ch 1, **join** (see Pattern Notes) in first st.

Rnd 2: Sl st in each st to ch-2 sp of first shell, **beg ch-2 shell** (see Special Stitches) in same sp, *ch 2, sc in next ch-4 sp, [ch 4, sc in next ch-4 sp] 5 times, ch 2, ch-2 shell in next shell, ch 2, sk next 2 dc of shell**, dc in next dc, ch 2, ch-2 shell in next shell, rep from * around, ending last rep at **, overlapping left side of back over right side, dc in first and last st of previous rnd at same time, ch 2, join in 3rd ch of beg ch-3.

Rnd 3: Sl st in each st to ch-2 sp of beg ch-2 shell, beg ch-2 shell in same sp, *ch 2, sc in next ch-4 sp, [ch 4, sc in next ch-4 sp] 4 times, ch 2, ch-2 shell in next shell, ch 2, sk next 2 dc of next shell, **V-st** *(see Special Stitches)* in next dc, ch 2**, ch-2 shell in next shell, rep from * around, ending last rep at **, join in 3rd ch of beg ch-3.

Rnd 4: Sl st in each st to ch-2 sp of beg ch-2 shell, beg ch-2 shell in same sp, *ch 2, sc in next ch-4 sp, [ch 4, sc in next ch-4 sp] 3 times, ch 2, ch-2 shell in next shell, ch 2, 7 dc in ch-4 sp of next V-st, ch 2**, ch-2 shell in next shell, rep from * around, ending last rep at **, join in 3rd ch of beg ch-3.

Rnd 5: Sl st in each st to ch-2 sp of beg ch-2 shell, beg ch-2 shell in same sp, *ch 2, sc in next ch-4 sp, [ch 4, sc in next ch-4 sp] twice, ch 2, ch-2 shell in next shell, ch 2, sk next 2 dc of shell, dc in first dc of next 7-dc group, [ch 1, dc in next dc] 6 times, ch 2**, ch-2 shell in next shell, rep from * around, ending last rep at **, join in 3rd ch of beg ch-3.

Rnd 6: Sl st in each st to ch-2 sp of beg ch-2 shell, beg ch-2 shell in same sp, *ch 2, sc in next ch-4 sp, ch 4, sc in next ch-4 sp, ch 2, ch-2 shell in next shell, ch 2, sk next 2 dc of next shell, sc in next dc, [ch 4, sc in next dc] 6 times, ch 2**, ch-2 shell in next shell, rep from * around, ending last rep at **, join in 3rd ch of beg ch-3.

Rnd 7: Sl st in each st to ch-2 sp of beg ch-2 shell, beg ch-2 shell in same sp, *ch 2, sc in next ch-4 sp, ch 2, ch-2 shell in next shell, ch 2, sc in next ch-4 sp, [ch 4, sc in next ch-4 sp] 5 times, ch 2**, ch-2 shell in next shell, rep from * around, ending last rep at **, join in 3rd ch of beg ch-3.

Rnd 8: Sl st in each st to ch-2 sp of beg ch-2 shell, beg ch-2 shell in same sp, *ch 2, dc in next sc, ch 2, ch-2 shell in next shell, ch 2, sc in next ch-4 sp, [ch 4, sc in next ch-4 sp] 4 times, ch 2**, ch-2 shell in next shell, rep from * around, ending last rep at **, join in 3rd ch of beg ch-3.

Rnd 9: Sl st in each st to ch-2 sp of beg ch-2 shell, beg ch-2 shell in same sp, *ch 2, sk next 2 dc of next shell, V-st in next dc, ch 2, ch-2 shell in next shell, ch 2, sc in next ch-4 sp, [ch 4, sc in next ch-4 sp] 3 times, ch 2**, ch-2 shell in next shell, rep from * around, ending last rep at **, join in 3rd ch of beg ch-3.

Rnd 10: Sl st in each st to ch-2 sp of beg ch-2 shell, beg ch-2 shell in same sp, *ch 2, 7 dc in next V-st, ch 2, ch-2 shell in next shell, ch 2, sc in next ch-4 sp, [ch 4, sc in next ch-4 sp] twice, ch 2**, ch-2 shell in next shell, rep from * around, ending last rep at **, join in 3rd ch of beg ch-3.

Rnd 11: Sl st in each st to ch-2 sp of beg ch-2 shell, beg ch-2 shell in same sp, *ch 2, sk next 2 dc of shell, dc in first dc of next 7-dc group, [ch 1, dc in next dc] 6 times, ch 2, ch-2 shell in next shell, ch2, sc in next ch-4 sp, ch 2**, ch-2 shell in next shell, rep from * around, ending last rep at **, join in 3rd ch of beg ch-3.

Rnd 12: Sl st in each st to ch-2 sp of beg ch-2 shell, beg ch-2 shell in same sp, *ch 2, sk next 2 dc of shell, sc in next dc, [ch 4, sc in next dc] 6 times, ch 2, ch-2 shell in next shell, ch2, sc in next ch-4 sp, ch 2**, ch-2 shell in next shell, rep from * around, ending last rep at **, join in 3rd ch of beg ch-3.

Rnd 13: Sl st in each st to ch-2 sp of beg ch-2 shell, beg ch-2 shell in same sp, *ch 2, sc in next ch-4 sp, [ch 4, sc in next ch-4 sp] 5 times, ch 2, ch-2 shell in next shell, ch2, dc in next sc, ch 2**, ch-2 shell in next shell, rep from * around, ending last rep at **, join in 3rd ch of beg ch-3.

Rnds 14–18: Rep rnds 3–7.

Rnd 19: Sl st in each st to ch-2 sp of beg ch-2 shell, ch 3, 5 dc in same sp as beg ch-3, *ch 2, dc in next sc, ch 2, 6 dc in ch-2 sp of next shell, ch 2, sc in next ch-4 sp, [ch 4, sc in next ch-4 sp] 4 times, ch 2**, 6 dc in ch-2 sp of next shell, rep from * around, ending last rep at **, join in 3rd ch of beg ch-3.

RUFFLE

Rnd 20: Ch 1, sc in same st as beg ch-1, sc in each of next 5 dc, *2 sc in next ch-2 sp, sc in next dc, 2 sc in next ch-2 sp, sc in each of next 6 dc, 2 sc in next ch-2 sp, 4 sc in each of next 4 ch-4 sps, 2 sc in next ch-2 sp **, sc in each of next 6 dc, rep from * around, ending last rep at **, join in first sc. (370 sc)

Rnd 21: Ch 1, sc in same sc as beg ch-1, *ch 5, sk next sc, sc in next sc, rep from * around, ch 2, join with dc in first sc. (185 sps)

Rnds 22–25: Ch 1, sc in sp formed by joining dc, *ch 5, sc in next ch-5 sp, rep from * around, ch 2, join with dc in first sc.

Rnd 26: Ch 1, sc in sp formed by joining dc, *ch 3, (**3-dc cl**—see Special Stitches, **picot**—see Special Stitches, 3-dc cl) in next ch-5 sp, ch 3, sc in next ch-5 sp**, [ch 5, sc in next ch-5 sp] 3 times, rep from * around, ending last rep at **, [ch 5, sc in next ch-5 sp] twice, ch 5, join in first sc. Fasten off.

SLEEVES

Rnd 1 (RS): With RS facing, join yarn with sc in 3rd ch of 1 underarm ch-5, ch 5, sc in next ch-2 sp, ch 5, sc around post of next dc (this dc will appear horizontal), ch 5, sc in next corner ch-2 sp on row 9 (already worked into), ch 5, *sc in center of next shell, ch 5, sc in next sp between shells, ch 5, rep from * 7 times, sc in center of next shell, ch 5, sc in next corner ch-2 sp on row 9 (already worked into), ch 5, sc around post of next dc (this dc will appear horizontal), ch 5, sc in next ch-2 sp, ch 2, join with dc in first sc. (24 sps)

Rnds 2–6: Ch 1, sc in sp formed by joining dc, *ch 5, sc in next ch-5 sp, rep from * around, ch 2, join with dc in first sc.

Rnd 7: Ch 1, sc in sp formed by joining dc, *ch 3, (3-dc cl, picot, 3-dc cl) in next ch-5 sp, ch 3**, sc in next ch-5 sp, rep from * around, ending last rep at **, join in first sc. Fasten off.

Work other Sleeve in same manner.

NECK EDGING

With RS facing, join yarn with sc in top right neck edge corner, *ch 3, sk next st, sc in next

st, rep from * around neck edge. Do not work down vertical back opening. Fasten off.

FINISHING

Cut a 38 [42]-inch length of ribbon. Weave ribbon through Dress just below underarm and tie in a bow.

Cut 2 (15 [17]-inch) lengths of ribbon. Weave ribbons though rnd 6 of each Sleeve and tie in a bow.

Sew snaps to back opening, evenly sp.

Sew 1 ribbon rose to center front neck.

HAT

Rnd 1 (RS): Ch 6, **join** (see Pattern Notes) in first ch to form ring, **ch 3** (see Pattern Notes), 19 dc in ring, join in 3rd ch of beg ch-3. (20 dc)

Rnds 2 & 3: Ch 3, 2 dc in next st, *dc in next st, 2 dc in next st, rep from * around, join in 3rd ch of beg ch-3. (45 dc at end of last rnd)

Rnd 4: Ch 3, dc in next st, 2 dc in next st, *dc in each of next 2 sts, 2 dc in next st, rep from * around, join in 3rd ch of beg ch-3. (60 dc)

Rnd 5: **Beg ch-2 shell** (see Special Stitches) in same ch as join, sk next 3 dc, *ch-2 shell (see Special Stitches) in next dc, sk next 3 dc, rep from * around, join in 3rd ch of beg ch-3. (15 ch-2 shells)

Rnd 6: Sl st in each st to ch-2 sp of beg ch-2 shell, beg ch-2 shell in same sp, *ch 1, ch-2 shell in next shell, ch 1, (2 dc, ch 4, 2 dc) in ch-2 sp of next shell, ch 1**, ch-2 shell in next shell, rep from * around, ending last rep at **, join in 3rd ch of beg ch-3. (5 ch-4 sps)

Rnd 7: Sl st in each st to ch-2 sp of beg ch-2 shell, beg ch-2 shell in same sp, *ch 1, ch-2 shell in next shell, ch 1, 7 dc in next ch-4 sp, ch 1**, ch-2 shell in next shell, rep from * around, ending last rep at **, join in 3rd ch of beg ch-3.

Rnd 8: Sl st in each st to ch-2 sp of beg ch-2 shell, beg ch-2 shell in same sp, *ch 1, ch-2 shell in next shell, ch 1, sk next 2 dc of shell, dc in first dc of next 7-dc group, [ch 1, dc in next dc] 6 times, ch 1**, ch-2 shell in next shell, rep from * around, ending last rep at **, join in 3rd ch of beg ch-3.

Rnd 9: Sl st in each st to ch-2 sp of beg ch-2 shell, beg ch-2 shell in same sp, *ch 1, dc in next ch-1 sp, ch-2 shell in next shell, ch 1, sk next 2 dc of shell, sc in next dc, [ch 4, sc in next dc] 6 times, ch 1**, ch-2 shell in next shell, rep from * around, ending last rep at **, join in 3rd ch of beg ch-3.

Rnd 10: Sl st in each st to ch-2 sp of beg ch-2 shell, beg ch-2 shell in same sp, *ch 1, **V-st** (see Special Stitches) in next dc, ch 1, ch-2 shell in next shell, ch 1, sc in next ch-4 sp, [ch 4, sc in next ch-4 sp] 5 times, ch 1**, ch-2 shell in next shell, rep from * around, ending last rep at **, join in 3rd ch of beg ch-3.

Rnd 11: Sl st in each st to ch-2 sp of beg ch-2 shell, beg shell in same sp, *ch 1, 7 dc in ch-4 sp of next V-st, ch 1, ch-2 shell in next shell, ch 1, sc in next ch-4 sp, [ch 4, sc in next ch-4 sp] 4 times, ch 1**, ch-2 shell in next shell, rep from * around, ending last rep at **, join in 3rd ch of beg ch-3.

Rnd 12: Sl st in each st to ch-2 sp of beg ch-2 shell, beg ch-2 shell in same sp, *ch 1, sk next 2 dc of shell, dc in first dc of next 7-dc group, [ch 1, dc in next dc] 6 times, ch 1, ch-2 shell in next shell, ch 1, sc in next ch-4 sp, [ch 4, sc in next ch-4 sp] 3 times, ch 1**, ch-2 shell in next shell, rep from * around, ending last rep at **, join in 3rd ch of beg ch-3.

Rnd 13: Sl st in each st to ch-2 sp of beg ch-2 shell, beg ch-2 shell in same sp, *ch 1, sk next 2 dc of shell, sc in next dc, [ch 4, sc in next dc]

6 times, ch 1, ch-2 shell in next shell, ch 1, sc in next ch-4 sp, [ch 4, sc in next ch-4 sp] twice, ch 1**, ch-2 shell in next shell, rep from * around, ending last rep at **, join in 3rd ch of beg ch-3.

Rnd 14: Sl st in each st to ch-2 sp of beg ch-2 shell, beg ch -2 shell in same sp, *ch 1, sc in next ch-4 sp, [ch 4, sc in next ch-4 sp] 5 times, ch 1, ch-2 shell in next shell, ch 1, sc in next ch-4 sp, ch 4, sc in next ch-4 sp, ch 1**, ch-2 shell in next shell, rep from * around, ending last rep at **, join in 3rd ch of beg ch-3.

Rnd 15: Sl st in each st to ch-2 sp of beg ch-2 shell, ch 3, 5 dc in same sp, * ch 1, sc in next ch-4 sp, [ch 4, sc in next ch-4 sp] 4 times, ch 1, 6 dc in ch-2 sp of next shell, ch 1, sc in next ch-4 sp, ch 1**, 6 dc in ch-2 sp of next shell, rep from * around, ending last rep at **, join in 3rd ch of beg ch-3.

Rnd 16: Ch 1, sc in same ch as beg ch-1, sc in each of next 5 dc, *sc in next ch-1 sp, 4 sc in each of next 4 ch-4 sps, sc in next ch-1 sp, sc in each of next 6 dc, sc in next ch-1 sp, sc in next sc, sc in next ch-1 sp**, sc in each of next 2 dc, 2 sc in next dc, sc in each of next 3 dc, rep from * around, ending last rep at **, join in first sc. (168 sc)

Rnd 17: **Ch 4** (see Pattern Notes), sk next sc, *dc in next sc, ch 1, sk next sc, rep from * around, join in 3rd ch of beg ch-4. (84 sps)

Rnd 18: Ch 1, sc in same ch as beg ch-1, *ch 5, sc in next dc, rep from * around, ch 3, join with dc in first sc.

Rnds 19 & 20: Ch 1, sc in sp formed by joining dc, *ch 5, sc in next ch-5 sp, rep from * around, ch 2, join with dc in first sc.

Rnd 21: Ch 1, sc in sp formed by joining dc, *ch 3, (**3-dc cl**—see Special Stitches, **picot**—see Special Stitches, 3-dc cl) in next ch-5 sp, ch 3, sc in next ch-5 sp**, [ch 5, sc in next ch-5 sp] twice, rep from * around, ending last rep at **, ch 5, sc in next ch-5 sp, ch 5, join in first sc. Fasten off.

FINISHING

Cut a 28 [30]-inch length of ribbon. Weave ribbon through rnd 17 of Hat and tie in a bow.

Sew 1 ribbon rose to top of Hat. ∎

Lacy Lemon Drop
Dress

SKILL LEVEL

EASY

FINISHED SIZE
6–9 months

FINISHED MEASUREMENTS
Chest: 22 inches

Length: 13½ inches

MATERIALS
- Red Heart Baby TLC medium (worsted) weight acrylic yarn (5 oz/358 yds/141g per skein):
    2 skeins #5322 powder yellow
- Light (light worsted) weight acrylic/nylon yarn (6 oz/430 yds/170g per skein):
    1 skein yellow/white/blue/red variegated
- Size C/2/2.75mm crochet hook or size needed to obtain gauge
- Tapestry needle
- Sewing needle
- 2 snaps
- Matching sewing thread

GAUGE
26 dc = 4 inches

PATTERN NOTES
Weave in ends as work progresses.

Chain-3 at beginning of row or round counts as double crochet unless otherwise stated.

Join with slip stitch as indicated unless otherwise stated.

Chain-5 at beginning of round counts as double crochet and chain-2 unless otherwise stated.

SPECIAL STITCHES
V-stitch (V-st): (Dc, ch 2, dc) in indicated st or sp.

Shell: (Cl—*see Special Stitches,* ch 3, cl) in indicated st or sp.

Cluster (cl): Holding back last lp of each dc on hook, 3 dc in indicated st or sp, yo and draw through all 4 lps on hook.

DRESS
YOKE
Row 1 (WS): With yellow, ch 72, sc in 2nd ch from hook, sc in each rem ch across, turn. *(71 sc)*

Row 2: Ch 3 *(see Pattern Notes)*, dc in each sc across, working 2 dc in each of 14 evenly sp sc, **changing color** *(see Stitch Guide)* to variegated in last st, turn. *(85 dc)*

Row 3: Ch 1, sc in first dc, *(tr, sl st) in next dc, sc in next dc, rep from * across, turn. *(42 tr, 43 sc)*

Row 4: Ch 3, dc in each tr and sc across, inc 12 dc evenly sp, turn. *(97 dc)*

Row 5: Rep row 3. *(48 tr, 49 sc)*

Row 6: Ch 3, dc in each tr and sc across, inc 10 dc evenly sp, turn. *(107 dc)*

Row 7: Rep row 3, changing color to yellow in last st. *(53 tr)*

Row 8: Ch 3, dc in each tr and sc across, inc 20 dc evenly sp, turn. *(127 dc)*

Row 9: Ch 1, sc in each st across, inc 22 sc evenly sp, turn. *(149 sc)*

Row 10: Ch 3, dc in each st across, inc 22 dc evenly sp, turn. *(171 dc)*

Row 11: Ch 3, dc in each of next 2 sts, ch 2, sk next 2 sts, *V-st *(see Special Stitches)* in next st, ch 2, sk next 2 sts, dc in each of next 3 sts**, ch 2, sk next 2 sts, rep from * across, ending last rep at **, turn. *(21 V-sts)*

Rnd 12 (RS): Now working in rnds, ch 3, dc in each of next 2 dc, *ch 2, **shell** *(see Special Stitches)* in ch-2 sp of next V-st, ch 2, sk next ch-2 sp, dc in each of next 3 dc, rep from * around, ch 2, **join** *(see Pattern Notes)* in 3rd ch of beg ch-3. *(21 shells)*

BODY

Rnd 1: Ch 3, dc in each of next 2 dc, [ch 2, shell in ch-3 sp of next shell, ch 2, dc in each of next 3 dc] 3 times, ch 5, sk next 5 shells, dc in each of next 3 dc, [ch 2, shell in ch-3 sp of next shell, ch 2, dc in each of next 3 dc] 5 times, ch 5, sk next 5 shells, dc in each of next 3 dc, [ch 2, shell in ch-3 sp of next shell, ch 2, dc in each of next 3 dc] 3 times, ch 2, V-st in last ch-2 sp, ch 2, join in 3rd ch of beg ch-3.

Rnd 2: Ch 3, 2 dc in next dc, dc in next dc, [ch 2, shell in next shell, ch 2, dc in next dc, 2 dc in next dc, dc in next dc] 3 times, ch 2, V-st in 3rd ch of next ch-5 sp, ch 2, dc in next dc, 2 dc in next dc, dc in next dc, [ch 2, shell in next shell, ch 2, dc in next dc, 2 dc in next dc, dc in next dc] 5 times, ch 2, V-st in 3rd ch of next ch-5 sp, ch 2, dc in next dc, 2 dc in next dc, dc in next dc, work [ch 2, shell in next shell, ch 2, dc in next dc, 2 dc in next dc, dc in next dc] 3 times, ch 2, shell in last V-st, ch 2, join in 3rd ch of beg ch-3.

Rnd 3: Ch 3, dc in each of next 3 dc, [ch 2, shell in next shell, ch 2, dc in each of next 4 dc] 3 times, ch 2, shell in next V-st, ch 2, sk next ch-2 sp, dc in each of next 4 dc, [ch 2, shell in next shell, ch 2, dc in each of next 4 dc] 5 times, ch 2, shell in next V-st, ch 2, sk next ch-2 sp, dc in each of next 4 dc, [ch 2, shell in next shell, ch 2, dc in each of next 4 dc] 3 times, ch 2, shell in last shell, ch 2, join in 3rd ch of beg ch-3.

Rnds 4 & 5: Ch 3, dc in each of next 3 dc, [ch 2, shell in next shell, ch 2, dc in each of next 4 dc] 13 times, ch 2, shell in next shell, ch 2, join in 3rd ch of beg ch-3.

Rnd 6: Ch 3, 2 dc in next dc, dc in each of next 2 dc, [ch 2, shell in next shell, ch 2, dc in next dc, 2 dc in next dc, dc in each of next 2 dc] 13 times, ch 2, shell in next shell, ch 2, join in 3rd ch of beg ch-3.

Rnd 7: Ch 3, dc in each of next 4 dc, [ch 2, shell in next shell, ch 2, dc in each of next 5 dc] 13 times, ch 2, shell in next shell, ch 2, join in 3rd ch of beg ch-3.

Rnd 8: Ch 3, dc in next dc, 2 dc in next dc, dc in each of next 2 dc, [ch 2, shell in next shell, ch 2, dc in each of next 2 dc, 2 dc in next dc, dc in each of next 2 dc] 13 times, ch 2, shell in next shell, ch 2, join in 3rd ch of beg ch-3.

Rnd 9: Ch 3, dc in each of next 2 dc, ch 2, dc in each of next 3 dc, [ch 3, shell in next shell, ch 3, dc in each of next 3 dc, ch 2, dc in each of next 3 dc] 13 times, ch 3, shell in next shell, ch 3, join in 3rd ch of beg ch-3.

Rnd 10: Ch 3, dc in each of next 2 dc, ch 2, sc in next ch-2 sp, ch 2, dc in each of next 3 dc, [ch 3, shell in next shell, ch 3, dc in each of next 3 dc, ch 2, sc in next ch-2 sp, ch 2, dc in each of next 3 dc] 13 times, ch 3, shell in next shell, ch 3, join in 3rd ch of beg ch-3.

Rnd 11: Ch 3, dc in each of next 2 dc, ch 2, sc in next ch-2 sp, ch 3, sc in next ch-2 sp, ch 2, dc in each of next 3 dc, [ch 3, shell in next shell, ch 3, dc in each of next 3 dc, ch 2, sc in next ch-2 sp, ch 3, sc in next ch-2 sp, ch 2, dc in each of next 3 dc] 13 times, ch 3, shell in next shell, ch 3, join in 3rd ch of beg ch-3.

Rnd 12: Ch 3, dc in each of next 2 dc, ch 2, shell in next ch-3 sp, ch 2, dc in each of next 3 dc, [ch 3, shell in next shell, ch 3, dc in each of next 3 dc, ch 2, shell in next ch-3 sp, ch 2, dc in each of next 3 dc] 13 times, ch 3, shell in next shell, ch 3, join in 3rd ch of beg ch-3.

Rnd 13: Ch 3, dc in each of next 2 dc, [ch 3, shell in next shell, ch 3, dc in each of next 3 dc]

25 times, ch 3, shell in next shell, ch 3, join in 3rd ch of beg ch-3.

Rnds 14 & 15: Rep rnd 13. At end of rnd 15, change color to variegated by drawing lp through.

Rnds 16 & 17: Rep rnd 13.

Rnd 18: Ch 2, **dc dec** (*see Stitch Guide*) in next 2 dc, *ch 3, (cl, ch 3, cl, ch 3, cl) in next shell, ch 3**, dc dec in next 3 dc, rep from * around, ending last rep at **, join in first st.

Rnd 19: Ch 1, sc in same st as beg ch-1, *ch 4, sk next ch-3 sp, shell in next ch-3 sp, ch 3, shell in next ch-3 sp, ch 4, sk next ch-3 sp**, sc in next dc dec, rep from * around, ending last rep at **, join in first sc.

Rnd 20: Sl st in next ch-4 sp, ch 1, sc in same sp as beg ch-1, *ch 4, cl in next shell, ch 4, [cl, ch 4] twice in next ch-3 sp, cl in next shell, ch 4**, sc in each of next 2 ch-4 sps, rep from * around, ending last rep at **, sc in next ch-4 sp, join in first sc.

Rnd 21: Sl st in each of first 3 chs of next ch-4 sp, ch 1, sc in same ch-4 sp, ch 5, *sc in next ch-4 sp, ch 5, rep from * around, join in first sc. Fasten off.

SLEEVE
Rnd 1: With RS facing, join yarn at center st of 1 underarm ch-5, **ch 5** (*see Pattern Notes*), dc in same st as beg ch-5, ch 2, 3 dc around post of next dc (*this dc will appear horizontal*), [ch 2, shell in next shell, ch 2, dc in each of next 3 dc] 4 times, ch 2, shell in next shell, ch 2, 3 dc around post of next dc (*this dc will appear horizontal*), ch 2, join in 3rd ch of beg ch-5.

Rnds 2 & 3: Sl st in next ch-2 sp, ch 5, dc in same sp as beg ch-5, [ch 2, dc in each of next 3 dc, ch 2, shell in next shell] 5 times, ch 2, dc in each of next 3 dc, ch 2, join in 3rd ch of beg ch-5.

Rnd 4: Sl st in next ch-2 sp, ch 1, 3 sc in same sp as beg ch-1, sk next ch sp, sc in each of next 3 dc, [3 sc in ch-3 sp of next shell, sk next ch sp, sc in each of next 3 dc] 5 times, join in first sc. (*36 sc*)

Rnd 5: Ch 1, sc in each sc around, join in first sc.

Rnd 6: Sl st in each sc around, join in joining sl st.

Rep for rem armhole.

NECK EDGING
Hold Dress with RS of back facing and foundation ch of Yoke at top, join yarn in unused lp of first ch of foundation ch, working in rem unused lps of chs, sl st in each ch around neck edge. Fasten off.

FINISHING
Sew snaps at back opening. ■

Katie-Belle
Dress & Floppy Hat

SKILL LEVEL

EASY

FINISHED SIZES
Instructions are written the same for sizes 6–9 months and 12–18 months. Different measurements are achieved by using the yarn and gauge indicated for each size. Changes for larger size are in [].

FINISHED MEASUREMENTS
DRESS
Chest: 22 [25] inches
Length: 15 [17] inches

HAT
Circumference: 18 [20½] inches
Length: 7½ [8½] inches

MATERIALS
6–9 MONTHS SIZE
- Red Heart Baby TLC light (DK) weight acrylic yarn (5 oz/358 yds/ 141g per skein):
    2 skeins #5737 powder pink
    1 skein #5011 white
- Size C/2/2.75mm crochet hook or size needed to obtain gauge
- 2¾ yds ¼–½-inch-wide ribbon

12–18 MONTHS SIZE
- Bernat Softee Baby light (light worsted) weight acrylic yarn (5 oz/ 362 yds/140g per skein):
    2 skeins #02001 pink
    1 skein #02000 white
- Size D/3/3.25mm crochet hook or size needed to obtain gauge
- 3 yds ¼–½-inch-wide ribbon

FOR BOTH SIZES
- Tapestry needle
- Sewing needle
- 2 snaps
- Matching thread

GAUGES
6–9 months size: 24 dc = 4 inches

12–18 months size: 21 dc = 4 inches

PATTERN NOTES
Weave in ends as work progresses.

Chain-4 at beginning of row counts as double crochet and chain-1 unless otherwise stated.

Chain-3 at beginning of row or round counts as double crochet unless otherwise stated.

Join with slip stitch as indicated unless otherwise stated.

DRESS
YOKE
Row 1 (RS): With pink, ch 82, sc in 2nd ch from hook, sc in each of next 12 chs, 3 sc in next ch *(first corner)*, sc in each of next 13 chs, 3 sc in next ch *(2nd corner made)*, sc in each of next 25 chs, 3 sc in next ch *(3rd corner made)*, sc in each of next 13 sc, 3 sc in next ch *(4th corner made)*, sc in each of last 13 chs, turn. *(89 sc)*

Row 2: **Ch 4** *(see Pattern Notes)*, sk next st, *[dc in next st, ch 1, sk next st] across to 2nd st of next corner, (dc, ch 2, dc) in 2nd st, ch 1, sk next st, rep from * 3 times, [dc in next st, ch 1, sk next st] across to last st, dc in last st, turn. *(48 ch sps)*

Row 3: **Ch 3** (*see Pattern Notes*), *[dc in next ch sp, dc in next dc] across to next corner ch-2 sp, 3 dc in corner ch-2 sp, dc in next dc, rep from * 3 times, [dc in next ch sp, dc in next dc] across to last st, dc in last st, turn. (*105 dc*)

Row 4: Ch 4, sk next st, *[dc in next st, ch 1, sk next st] across to 2nd st of next corner, (dc, ch 2, dc) in 2nd st, ch 1, sk next st, rep from * 3 times, [dc in next st, ch 1, sk next st] across to last st, dc in last st, turn. (*56 ch sps*)

Rows 5–10: [Rep rows 3 and 4 alternately] 3 times. (*80 ch sps at end of last row*)

BODY

Rnd 1 (RS): Now working in rnds, ch 3, [dc in next ch sp, dc in next dc] 11 times, dc in next corner ch sp, ch 7 (*underarm made*), sk next 16 ch sps, dc in next corner ch sp, dc in next dc, [dc in next ch sp, dc in next dc] 22 times, dc in next corner ch sp, ch 7 (*underarm made*), sk next 16 ch sps, dc in next corner ch sp, [dc in next dc, dc in next ch sp] 11 times, dc in last dc. ch 1, **join** (*see Pattern Notes*) in 3rd ch of beg ch-3. **Do not turn.** (*95 dc*)

Rnd 2: Ch 4, sk next st, *dc in next st, ch 1, sk next st, rep from * around working in all dc and underarm chs, dc in last ch-1 sp, ch 1, join in 3rd ch of beg ch-4. (*55 ch sps*)

Rnd 3: Sl st in next ch sp, ch 3, 4 dc in same sp as beg ch-3, sk next ch sp, *5 dc in next ch sp, sk next ch sp, rep from * around, join in 3rd ch of beg ch-3, turn. (*28 5-dc groups*)

Rnd 4: Sc in each of next 2 sts, [3 sc in next st (*center st of 5-dc group*), sc in each of next 4 sts] 27 times, 3 sc in next st, sc in each of last 2 sts, join in first sc, turn. (*196 sc*)

Rnd 5: Working in **back lps** (*see Stitch Guide*), sl st in each of next 2 sts, ch 3, dc in next st, 3 dc in next st (*center st of 3-sc group*), dc in each of next 2 sts, sk next 2 sts, [dc in each of next 2 sts, 3 dc in next st, dc in each of next 2 sts, sk next 2 sts] 27 times, join in 3rd ch of beg ch-3, turn.

Rnd 6: Sc in each of next 3 sts, [3 sc in next st (*center st of 3-dc group*), sc in each of next 6 sts] 27 times, 3 sc in next st, sc in each of last 3 sts, join in first sc, turn. (*252 sc*)

Rnd 7: Working in back lps, sl st in each of next 2 sts, ch 3, dc in each of next 2 sts, 3 dc in next st (*center st of 3-sc group*), dc in each of next 3 sts, sk next 2 sts, [dc in each of next 3 sts, 3 dc in next st, dc in each of next 3 sts, sk next 2 sts] 27 times, join in 3rd ch of beg ch-3, turn. (*252 dc*)

Rnd 8: Sc in each of next 4 sts, [3 sc in next st (*center st of 3-dc group*), sc in each of next 8 sts] 27 times, 3 sc in next st, sc in each of last 4 sts, join in beg sc, turn. (*308 sc*)

Rnd 9: Working in back lps, sl st in each of next 2 sts, ch 3, dc in each of next 3 sts, 3 dc in next st (*center st of 3-sc group*), dc in each of next 4 sts, sk next 2 sts, [dc in each of next 4 sts, 3 dc in next st, dc in each of next 4 sts, sk next 2 sts] 27 times, join in 3rd ch of beg ch-3, turn. (*308 dc*)

Rnd 10: Sc in each of next 5 sts, [3 sc in next st (*center st of 3-dc group*), sc in each of next 10 sts] 27 times, 3 sc in next st, sc in each of last 5 sts, join in beg sc, turn. (*364 sc*)

Rnd 11: Working in back lps, sl st in each of next 2 sts, ch 3, dc in each of next 4 sts, 3 dc in next st (*center st of 3-sc group*), dc in each of next 5 sts, sk next 2 sts, [dc in each of next 5 sts, 3 dc in next st, dc in each of next 5 sts, sk next 2 sts] 27 times, join in 3rd ch of beg ch-3, turn. (*364 dc*)

Rnd 12: Sc in each of next 6 sts, [3 sc in next st (*center st of 3-dc group*), sc in each of next 12 sts] 27 times, 3 sc in next st, sc in each of last 6 sts, join in beg sc, turn. (*420 sc*)

Rnd 13: Working in back lps, sl st in each of next 2 sts, ch 3, dc in each of next 5 sts, 3 dc in next st (*center st of 3-sc group*), dc in each of next 6 sts, sk next 2 sts, [dc in each of next 6 sts, 3 dc in next st, dc in each of next 6 sts, sk next 2 sts] 27 times, join in 3rd ch of beg ch-3, turn. (*420 dc*)

Rnd 14: Sc in each of next 7 sts, [3 sc in next st (*center st of 3-dc group*), sc in each of next 14 sts] 27 times, 3 sc in next st, sc in each of last 7 sts, join in beg sc, turn. (*476 sc*)

Rnd 15: Working in back lps, sl st in each of next 2 sts, ch 3, dc in each of next 6 sts, 3 dc in next st (*center st of 3-sc group*), dc in each of next 7 sts, sk next 2 sts, [dc in each of next 7 sts, 3 dc in

next st, dc in each of next 7 sts, sk next 2 sts] 27 times, join in 3rd ch of beg ch-3, turn. *(476 dc)*

Rnd 16: Sc in each of next 8 sts, [3 sc in next st *(center st of 3-dc group)*, sc in each of next 16 sts] 27 times, 3 sc in next st, sc in each of last 8 sts, join in beg sc, turn. *(532 sc)*

Rnd 17: Working in back lps, sl st in each of next 2 sts, ch 3, dc in each of next 7 sts, 3 dc in next st *(center st of 3-sc group)*, dc in each of next 8 sts, sk next 2 sts, [dc in each of next 8 sts, 3 dc in next st, dc in each of next 8 sts, sk next 2 sts] 27 times, join in 3rd ch of beg ch-3, turn. *(532 dc)*

Rnd 18: Sc in each of next 9 sts, [3 sc in next st *(center st of 3-dc group)*, sc in each of next 18 sts] 27 times, 3 sc in next st, sc in each of last 9 sts, join in beg sc, turn. *(588 sc)*

Rnd 19: Working in back lps, sl st in each of next 2 sts, ch 3, dc in each of next 8 sts, 3 dc in next st *(center st of 3-sc group)*, dc in each of next 9 sts, sk next 2 sts, [dc in each of next 9 sts, 3 dc in next st, dc in each of next 9 sts, sk next 2 sts] 27 times, join in 3rd ch of beg ch-3, turn. *(588 dc)*

Rnd 20: Sc in each of next 10 sts, [3 sc in next st *(center st of 3-dc group)*, sc in each of next 20 sts] 27 times, 3 sc in next st, sc in each of last 10 sts, join in beg sc, turn. *(644 sc)*

Rnd 21: Working in back lps, sl st in each of next 2 sts, ch 3, dc in each of next 9 sts, 3 dc in next st *(center st of 3-sc group)*, dc in each of next 10 sts, sk next 2 sts, [dc in each of next 10 sts, 3 dc in next st, dc in each of next 10 sts, sk next 2 sts] 27 times, join in 3rd ch of beg ch-3, changing to white by drawing lp through, fasten off pink, turn. *(644 dc)*

Rnd 22: Sc in each of next 11 sts, [3 sc in next st *(center st of 3-dc group)*, sc in each of next 22 sts] 27 times, 3 sc in next st, sc in each of last 11 sts, join in first sc, turn. *(700 sc)*

Rnd 23: Working in back lps, sl st in each of next 2 sts, ch 3, dc in each of next 10 sts, 3 dc in next st *(center st of 3-sc group)*, dc in each of next 11 sts, sk next 2 sts, [dc in each of next 11 sts, 3 dc in next st, dc in each of next 11 sts, sk next 2 sts] 27 times, join in 3rd ch of beg ch-3. **Do not turn.** *(700 dc)*

Rnd 24: Ch 1, sc in same ch as beg ch-1, *ch 3, sc in each of next 3 dc, rep from * around, join in first sc. Fasten off.

SLEEVE

Rnd 1 (RS): With RS facing, join pink in right-most corner sp of 1 underarm, ch 1, 2 sc in same sp as beg ch-1, sc around post of next dc *(this dc will appear horizontal)*, sc in each of next 4 ch sps, sc around post of next dc *(this dc will appear horizontal)*, sc in next corner sp of underarm, 5 dc in next ch sp, [sc in next ch sp, 5 dc in next ch sp] 4 times, sc in next dc, 5 dc in next ch sp, [sc in next ch sp, 5 dc in next ch sp] 3 times, join in first sc. *(9 5-dc groups)*

Rnd 2: Ch 1, [**sc dec** *(see Stitch Guide)* in next 2 sts] 4 times, sc in each of next 5 dc, [sk next sc, sc in each of next 5 dc] 8 times, join in first sc dec, changing to white by drawing lp through, fasten off pink.

Rnd 3: Ch 1, sc in same st as beg ch-1, *ch 3, sc in each of next 3 sc, rep from * around, join in first sc. Fasten off.

Work other Sleeve in same manner.

NECK EDGE TRIM

Row 1 (WS): With WS facing, join white at neck edge corner, ch 1, sc in same st as beg ch-1, sc in next st, sk next st, *sc in each of next 3 sts, sk next st, rep from * across to last 2 sts, sc in each of last 2 sts, turn.

Row 2 (RS): Ch 1, sc in each of first 2 sc, ch 3, *sc in each of next 3 sc, ch 3, rep from * across to last 2 sc, sc in each of last 2 sc. Fasten off.

FINISHING

Cut a 36 [40]-inch length of ribbon. Weave ribbon through dc row just below back joining and tie in a bow.

Cut 2 (14 [15]-inch) lengths of ribbon. Sew ribbon ends at each neck corner. Weave each ribbon through topmost dc row to center neck and tie in a bow.

Sew snaps to back opening.

FLOPPY HAT

Rnd 1 (RS): Ch 7, **join** (see Pattern Notes) in first ch to form ring, **ch 3** (see Pattern Notes), 23 dc in ring, join in 3rd ch of beg ch-3. (24 dc)

Rnds 2 & 3: Ch 3, 2 dc in next st, *dc in next st, 2 dc in next st, rep from * around, join in 3rd ch of beg ch-3. (54 dc at end of last rnd)

Rnd 4: **Ch 4** (see Pattern Notes), sk next st, *dc in next st, ch 1, sk next st, rep from * around, join in 3rd of beg ch-4. (27 ch sps)

Rnd 5: Ch 3, 3 dc in next ch sp, *dc in next dc, 2 dc in next ch sp, rep from * around, join in 3rd ch of beg ch-3. (82 dc)

Rnd 6: Rep rnd 4. (41 ch sps)

Rnd 7: Ch 3, dc in next ch sp, *dc in next dc, 2 dc in next ch sp, dc in next dc, dc in next ch sp, rep from * around, join in 3rd ch of beg ch-3. (102 dc)

Rnd 8: Rep rnd 4. (51 ch sps)

Rnd 9: Ch 3, 2 dc in next ch sp, dc in next dc, 2 dc in next ch sp, *dc in next dc, dc in next ch sp, rep from * around, join in 3rd ch of beg ch-3. (104 dc)

Rnd 10: Rep rnd 4. (52 ch sps)

Rnd 11: Ch 3, dc in next ch sp, *dc in next dc, dc in next ch sp, rep from * around, join in 3rd ch of beg ch-3. (104 dc)

Rnd 12: Rep rnd 4. (52 ch sps)

BRIM

Rnd 13: Sl st in next ch sp, ch 3, 4 dc in same sp, *sk next sp, 5 dc in next ch sp, rep from * around, join in 3rd ch of beg ch-3, turn. (26 5-dc groups)

Rnd 14: Sc in each of next 2 sts, [3 sc in next st (center st of 5-dc group), sc in each of next 4 sts] 25 times, 3 sc in next st, sc in each of last 2 sts, join in first sc, turn. (182 sc)

Rnd 15: Working in **back lps** (see Stitch Guide), sl st in each of next 2 sts, ch 3, dc in next st, 3 dc in next st (center st of 3-sc group), dc in each of next 2 sts, sk next 2 sts, [dc in each of next 2 sts, 3 dc in next st, dc in each of next 2 sts, sk next 2 sts] 27 times, join in 3rd ch of beg ch-3, turn. (182 dc)

Rnd 16: Sc in each of next 3 sts, [3 sc in next st (center st of 3-dc group), sc in each of next 6 sts] 25 times, 3 sc in next st, sc in each of last 3 sts, join in first sc, turn. (234 sc)

Rnd 17: Working in back lps, sl st in each of next 2 sts, ch 3, dc in each of next 2 sts, 3 dc in next st (center st of 3-sc group), dc in each of next 3 sts, sk next 2 sts, [dc in each of next 3 sts, 3 dc in next st, dc in each of next 3 sts, sk next 2 sts] 25 times, join in 3rd ch of beg ch-3, changing to white by drawing lp through, fasten off pink. **Do not turn.** (234 dc)

Rnd 18: Ch 1, sc in same ch as beg ch-1, sc in each of next 2 dc, ch 3, *sc in each of next 3 dc, ch 3, rep from * around, join in first sc. Fasten off.

FINISHING

Cut a 32 [35]-inch length of ribbon. Weave ribbon through rnd 12 of Hat and tie in a bow. ■

Ripple Stitch
Layette

SKILL LEVEL

EASY

FINISHED SIZES
Instructions are the same for sizes 0–6 months and 6–12 months. Different measurements are achieved by using the yarn, hook and gauge indicated for each size.

FINISHED MEASUREMENTS
SWEATER
Chest: 18½ [21¾] inches
Length: 11 [13] inches

BONNET
Circumference: 18 [21] inches
Length: 7½ [8¾] inches

BOOTIES
4½ [5¼] inches from toe to heel when flat

MATERIALS
SIZE 0–6 MONTHS
- Red Heart Baby TLC medium (worsted) weight acrylic yarn (5 oz/ 358 yds/141g per skein):
    2 skeins #5881 powder blue
- Size C/2/2.75mm crochet hook or size needed to obtain gauge
- 2¾ yds of ¼–½-inch-wide ribbon

SIZE 6–12 MONTHS
- Bernat Softee Baby light (light worsted) weight acrylic yarn (5 oz/ 362 yds/140g per skein):
    2 skeins #02002 pale blue
- Size D/3/3.25mm crochet hook or size needed to obtain gauge
- 3 yds ¼–½-inch-wide ribbon

FOR BOTH SIZES
- Tapestry needle
- Sewing needle
- 5 ribbon roses (optional)
- 2 snaps
- Matching sewing thread

GAUGE
Size C hook: 26 sc = 4 inches; 28 sc rows = 4 inches

Size D hook: 22 sc = 4 inches; 24 rows = 4 inches

PATTERN NOTES
Weave in ends as work progresses.

Chain-3 at beginning of row or round counts as double crochet unless otherwise stated.

Join with slip stitch as indicated unless otherwise stated.

Chain-4 at beginning of round counts as double crochet and chain-1 unless otherwise stated.

SWEATER
YOKE

Row 1 (WS): Ch 72, sc in 2nd ch from hook, sc in each rem ch across, turn. *(71 sc)*

Row 2: Ch 3 *(see Pattern Notes)*, dc in each of next 10 sc, 3 dc in next sc *(first corner made)*, dc in each of next 12 sc, 3 dc in next sc *(2nd corner made)*, dc in each of next 21 sc, 3 dc in next sc *(3rd corner made)*, dc in each of next 12 sc, 3 dc in next sc *(last corner made)*, dc in each of last 11 sc, turn. *(79 dc)*

Row 3: Ch 1, working in **back lps** *(see Stitch Guide)*, *sc in each st across to next corner st, 3 sc in corner st, rep from * 3 times, sc in each rem st across, turn. *(87 sc)*

Rows 4–18: Rep row 3. *(207 sc at end of last row)*

Row 19: Ch 1, working in back lps, *sc in each st to next corner st, 5 sc in corner st, rep from * 3 times, sc in each rem st across, turn. *(223 sc)*

BODY

Row 1 (RS): Ch 3, working in back lps, dc in each of next 2 sts, [sk next 2 sts, dc in each of next 2 sts, 3 dc in next st, dc in each of next 2 sts] 4 times, sk next 50 sts, dc in each of next 2 sts, 3 dc in next st, dc in each of next 2 sts, [sk next 2 sts, dc in each of next 2 sts, 3 dc in next st, dc in each of next 2 sts] 8 times, sk next 50 sts, dc in each of next 2 sts, 3 dc in next st, dc in each of next 2 sts, [sk next 2 sts, dc in each of next 2 sts, 3 dc in next st, dc in each of next 2 sts] 3 times, sk next 2 sts, dc in each of last 3 sts, turn. *(125 dc)*

Row 2: Ch 1, sc in first st, *sc in each st across to 2nd dc of next 3-dc group, 3 sc in 2nd dc, rep from * 16 times, sc in each rem st across, turn. *(159 sc)*

Row 3: Ch 3, working in back lps, dc in first 2 sc, *sk next 2 sc, dc in each of next 3 sc, 3 dc in next sc, dc in each of next 3 sc, rep from * across to last 4 sc, sk next 2 sc, dc in next sc, 2 dc in last sc, turn.

Row 4: Rep row 2. *(193 sc)*

Row 5: Ch 3, working in back lps, dc in first 2 sc, *sk next 2 sc, dc in each of next 4 sc, 3 dc in next sc, dc in each of next 4 sc, rep from * across to last 4 sc, sk next 2 sc, dc in next sc, 2 dc in last sc, turn.

Row 6: Rep row 2. *(227 sc)*

Row 7: Ch 3, working in back lps, ch 3, dc in first 2 sc, *sk next 2 sc, dc in each of next 5 sc, 3 dc in next sc, dc in each of next 5 sc, rep from * across to last 4 sc, sk next 2 sc, dc in next sc, 2 dc in last sc, turn.

Row 8: Rep row 2. *(261 sc)*

Row 9: Ch 3, working in back lps, dc in first 2 sc, *sk next 2 sts, dc in each of next 6 sc, 3 dc in next st, dc in each of next 6 sc, rep from * across to last 4 sc, sk next 2 sc, dc in next sc, 2 dc in last sc, turn.

Row 10: Rep row 2. *(295 sc)*

Row 11: Ch 3, working in back lps, dc in first 2 sc, *sk next 2 sts, dc in each of next 7 sc, 3 dc in next st, dc in each of next 7 sc, rep from * across to last 4 sc, sk next 2 sc, dc in next sc, 2 dc in last sc, turn.

Row 12: Rep row 2. *(329 sc)*

Row 13: Ch 3, working in back lps, dc in first 2 sc, *sk next 2 sts, dc in each of next 8 sc, 3 dc in next st, dc in each of next 8 sc, rep from * across to last 4 sc, sk next 2 sc, dc in next sc, 2 dc in last sc, turn.

Row 14: Rep row 2. *(363 sc)*

Row 15: Ch 3, working in back lps, dc in first 2 sc, *sk next 2 sts, dc in each of next 9 sc, 3 dc in next st, dc in each of next 9 sc, rep from * across to last 4 sc, sk next 2 sc, dc in next sc, 2 dc in last sc, turn.

Row 16: Rep row 2. *(397 sc)*

Row 17: Ch 3, working in back lps, dc in first 2 sc, *sk next 2 sts, dc in each of next 10 sc, 3 dc in next st, dc in each of next 10 sc, rep from * across to last 4 sc, sk next 2 sc, dc in next sc, 2 dc in last sc, turn.

Row 18: Rep row 2. *(431 sc)*

BOTTOM EDGING
Row 19: Ch 1, sc in first sc, *ch 3, sc in each of next 3 sc, rep from * across to last sc, ch 3, sc in last sc. Fasten off.

NECK EDGING
With RS facing, **join** *(see Pattern Notes)* yarn in top right corner, ch 1, sc in first st, *ch 3, sc in each of next 3 sts, rep from * across to last st, ch 3, sc in last st. Fasten off.

SLEEVES
Rnd 1 (RS): With RS facing, join yarn in back lp of last unworked st of one underarm, sl st in back lp of first unworked underarm st, ch 3, working in back lps, dc in next st, 3 dc in next st, dc in each of next 2 sts, sk next st, *dc in each of next 2 sts, 3 dc in next st, dc in each of next 2 sts, sk next st, rep from * 6 times, join in 3rd ch of beg ch-3, turn. *(56 dc)*

Rnd 2: Sk first st, sl st in each of next 2 sts, ch 1, sc in same st as beg ch-1, sc in next st, 3 sc in next st, sc in each of next 2 sts, sk next 2 sts, *sc in each of next 2 sts, 3 sc in next st, sc in each of next 2 sts, sk next 2 sts, rep from * 6 times, join in first sc, turn.

Rnd 3: Working in back lps, sk first st, sl st in each of next 2 sts, ch 3, dc in next st, 3 dc in next st, dc in each of next 2 sts, sk next 2 sts, *dc in each of next 2 sts, 3 dc in next st, dc in each of next 2 sts, sk next 2 sts, rep from * 6 times, join in 3rd ch of beg ch-3, turn.

Rep rnds 2 and 3 until piece measures 6 inches or to desired length. At end of last row, **do not turn.**

CUFF
Note: Work following rnds loosely to allow for ease in Cuff.

Rnd 1 (RS): Ch 1, sk next st, sc in each of next 3 sts, *sk next 4 sts, sc in each of next 3 sts, rep from * 6 times, sk next 2 sts, join in first sc. *(24 sc)*

Rnds 2 & 3: Ch 1, sc in each st around, join in first sc.

Rnd 4: Ch 1, sc in same sc as beg ch-1 and in next sc, ch 3, *sc in each of next 2 sts, ch 3, rep from * around, join in first sc. Fasten off.

Work other Sleeve in same manner.

FINISHING
Cut a 36 [39]-inch length of ribbon. Weave ribbon through sps of row 1 of Body and tie in a bow.

Sew snaps to tops of yoke fronts.

Sew 2 ribbon roses to outside of yoke, corresponding with snaps.

BONNET
Rnd 1 (WS): Ch 8, **join** *(see Pattern Notes)* in first ch to form ring, ch 1, 24 sc in ring, join in beg ch-1, turn. *(24 sc)*

Rnds 2–6: Ch 1, working in **back lps** *(see Stitch Guide)*, sc in each st, working 2 sc *(inc)* in each of 6 evenly sp sts around, join in beg ch-1, turn. *(54 sc)*

Rnds 7–11: Ch 1, working in **back lps** *(see Stitch Guide)*, sc in each st, inc 8 sts evenly sp around, join in beg ch-1, turn. *(94 sc)*

Rnd 12: Ch 1, working in back lps, sc in each st, inc 10 sts evenly sp around, join in beg ch-1, turn. *(104 sc)*

Rnd 13: Ch 1, working in back lps, sc in each st, inc 12 sts evenly sp around, join in beg ch-1, turn. *(116 sc)*

BODY
Row 14 (RS): Now working in rows, ch 3, working in back lps, dc in next st, sk next 2 sts, *dc in each of next 2 sts, 3 dc in next st, dc in each of next 2 sts, sk next 2 sts, rep from * 13 times, dc in each of next 2 sts, leaving rem sts unworked, turn. *(102 dc)*

Row 15: Ch 1, 2 sc in same st as beg ch-1, *sk next 2 sts, sc in each of next 2 sts, 3 sc in next st, sc in each of next 2 sts, rep from * across to last 3 sts, sk next 2 sts, 2 sc in last st, turn.

Row 16: Ch 3, working in back lps, dc in same st as beg ch-3, *sk next 2 sts, dc in each of next 2 sts, 3 dc in next st, dc in each of next 2 sts, rep from * across to last 3 sts, sk next 2 sts, 2 dc in last st, turn.

Rows 17–24: [Rep rows 15 and 16 alternately] 4 times.

Row 25: Rep row 15.

EDGING

Rnd 1 (RS): Ch 3, dc in each st across, working across edge of Body, work 16 sc evenly sp across, working across back neck edge, work 8 sc evenly sp across, working across next edge of Body, work 16 sc evenly sp to beg ch-3, join in 3rd ch of beg ch-3.

Rnd 2: Ch 1, sc in each of first 3 dc, *ch 3, sc in each of next 3 dc, rep from * across front edge, working around side and back and side of Bonnet, sc in each 40 sc, join in first sc. Fasten off.

FINISHING

Cut a 27 [30]-inch length of ribbon. Weave ribbon through bottom dc row of Bonnet for ties.

Sew ribbon rose to top center of Bonnet.

BOOTIE
MAKE 2.
CUFF

Rnd 1 (RS): Ch 36, being careful not to twist ch, **join** (see Pattern Notes) in first ch to form ring, **ch 4** (see Pattern Notes), sk next ch, *dc in next ch, ch 1, sk next ch, rep from * around, join in 3rd ch of beg ch-4. (18 ch sps)

Rnd 2: Ch 1, sc in same st as beg ch-1, sc in next ch-1 sp, *sc in next dc, sc in next ch-1 sp, rep from * around, join in **back lp** (see Pattern Notes) of first sc. (36 sc)

Rnd 3: **Ch 3** (see Pattern Notes), working in back lps, dc in next st, 3 dc in next st, dc in each of next 2 sts, sk next st, *dc in each of next 2 sts, 3 dc in next dc, dc in each of next 2 sts, sk next st, rep from * around, join in 3rd ch of beg ch-3, turn. (42 dc)

Rnd 4: Sk first st, sl st in each of next 2 sts, ch 1, sc in same st as beg ch-1, sc in next st, 3 sc in next st, sc in each of next 2 sts, sk next 2 sts, *sc in each of next 2 sts, 3 sc in next st, sc in each of next 2 sts, sk next 2 sts, rep from * around, join in first sc, turn.

Rnd 5: Working in back lps, sk first st, sl st in each of next 2 sts, ch 3, dc in next st, 3 dc in next st, dc in each of next 2 sts, sk next 2 sts, *dc in each of next 2 sts, 3 dc in next st, dc in each of next 2 sts, sk next 2 sts, rep from * around, join in 3rd ch of beg ch-3, turn.

Rnds 6 & 7: Rep rnds 4 and 5. At end of rnd 7, do not turn.

Rnd 8: Ch 1, sc in each of first 3 sts, ch 3, *sc in each of next 3 sts, ch 3, rep from * around, join in first sc. Fasten off.

INSTEP

Row 1 (RS): With RS facing and Cuff upside down, sk 6 dc from beg ch-4 of rnd 1 of Cuff, join yarn in next dc, ch 1, sc in same st as beg ch-1, [sc in next sp, sc in next st] 4 times, turn. *(9 sc)*

Rows 2–6: Ch 1, working in back lps, ch 1, sc in each sc across, turn. At end of last row, fasten off.

FOOT & SOLE

Rnd 1 (RS): With RS facing and Cuff upside down, join yarn in first ch of beg ch-36 ring, ch 1, sc in same st as beg ch-1, sc in next sp, [sc in next st, sc in next sp] 6 times, work 6 sc evenly sp across side edge of Instep to corner, 3 sc in corner, sc in back lp of each of next 9 sc, 3 sc in corner, 6 sc evenly sp across side edge of Instep, [sc in next sp, sc in next st] 6 times, sc in next sp, join in first sc, turn. *(54 sts)*

Rnds 2–6: Ch 1, working in back lps, ch 1, sc in each st around, join in beg ch-1, turn.

Rnd 7: Ch 1, working in back lps, ch 1, sc in same sc as beg ch-1, **sc dec** *(see Stitch Guide)* in next 2 sts, sc in each of next 16 sc, [sc dec in next 2 sts] twice, sc in each of next 9 sc, [sc dec in next 2 sts] twice, sc in each of next 16 sts, sc dec in last 2 sts, join in first sc, turn. *(48 sc)*

Rnd 8: Ch 1, working in back lps, sc in same sc as beg ch-1, [sc dec in next 2 sts] twice, sc in each of next 13 sts, [sc dec in next 2 sts] twice, sc in each of next 5 sts, [sc dec in next 2 sts] twice, sc in each of next 13 sts, [sc dec in next 2 sts] twice, join in first sc, turn. *(40 sc)*

Rnd 9: Ch 1, working in back lps, sc in same sc as beg ch-1, [sc dec in next 2 sts] twice, sc in each of next 14 sts, sc dec in next 3 sts, sc in each of next 14 sts, [sc dec in next 2 sts] twice, join in first sc. Leaving a 12-inch tail, fasten off. *(34 sc)*

FINISHING

Turn Booties inside out. With tapestry needle, sew openings closed.

Cut 2 (16 [18]-inch) lengths of ribbon. Weave ribbon through row 1 of each Cuff and tie in a bow.

Sew 1 ribbon rose to Instep of each Bootie. ∎

Apple Blossom
Dress

SKILL LEVEL

INTERMEDIATE

FINISHED SIZES
Instructions are the same for sizes 6–12 months and 12–18 months. Yarn and gauge determine size. Changes for larger size are in [ ].

FINISHED MEASUREMENTS
Chest: 21 [23] inches
Length: 14 [15¼] inches

MATERIALS
6–12 MONTHS SIZE
• Bernat Baby super fine (fingering) weight acrylic/nylon yarn (1¾ oz/ 191 yds/50g per skein):
  3 skeins #35469 pink

12–18 MONTHS SIZE
• Bernat Softee Baby light (light worsted) weight acrylic yarn (5 oz/ 362 yds/140g per skein):
  2 skeins #02001 pink

FOR BOTH SIZES
• Size C/2/2.75mm crochet hook or size needed to obtain gauge
• Tapestry needle
• Sewing needle
• 3 ribbon roses
• 3 snaps
• Matching sewing thread

GAUGE
With fingering-weight yarn: 24 dc = 4 inches

With light worsted-weight yarn: 22 dc = 4 inches

PATTERN NOTES
Weave in ends as work progresses.

Chain-3 at beginning of row or round counts as double crochet unless otherwise stated.

Join with slip stitch as indicated unless otherwise stated.

SPECIAL STITCHES
Beginning shell (beg shell): (Ch 3, dc, ch 2, 2 dc) in indicated st or sp.

Shell: (2 dc, ch 2, 2 dc) in indicated st or sp.

Picot shell: (Dc, **picot**—*see Special Stitches*, dc, ch 3, dc, picot, dc) in indicated st or sp.

Picot: Ch 4, hdc in first ch of ch-4.

Half picot shell: (Dc, picot, dc) in indicated st or sp.

3-double crochet cluster (3-dc cl): Holding back last lp of each dc on hook, 3 dc in indicated st or sp, yo and draw through all 4 lps on hook.

Beginning 3-double crochet shell (beg 3-dc shell): (Ch 3, 2 dc, ch 3, 3 dc) in indicated st or sp.

3-double crochet shell (3-dc shell): (3 dc, ch 3, 3 dc) in indicated st or sp.

Beginning 3-double crochet cluster (beg 3-dc cl): Ch 3, holding back last lp of each dc on hook, 3 dc in indicated st or sp, yo and draw through all 4 lps on hook.

DRESS
BODICE
Row 1 (WS): Ch 80, sc in 2nd ch from hook and in each ch across, turn. (*79 sc*)

Row 2: Ch 1, sc in each sc across, turn.

Row 3: Beg shell (*see Special Stitches*) in first sc, *sk next 2 sts, **shell** (*see Special Stitches*) in next st, rep from * across, turn. (*27 shells*)

Rows 4 & 5: Ch 3 (*see Pattern Notes*), shell in ch-2 sp of each shell across, turn.

Rows 6 & 7: Ch 3, shell in first shell, *ch 1, shell in next shell, rep from * across, turn.

Row 8: Ch 3, shell in first shell, *ch 2, shell in next shell, rep from * across, turn.

Row 9: Ch 3, (2 dc, ch 3, 2 dc) in first shell, *ch 3, (2 dc, ch 3, 2 dc) in next shell, rep from * across, turn.

Row 10: Ch 3, 7 dc in first ch-3 sp, *sc in next ch-3 sp, 7 dc in next ch-3 sp, rep from * across, dc in last st, turn.

BODY

Rnd 1 (WS): Now working in rnds, ch 3, (4 dc, ch 3, 4 dc) in 4th st of first 7-dc group, *ch 3, **picot shell** (*see Special Stitches*) in 4th st of next 7-dc group, ch 3, (4 dc, ch 3, 4 dc) in 4th st of next 7-dc group, rep from * around, ch 3, **join** (*see Pattern Notes*) in 3rd ch of beg ch-3, turn.

Rnd 1 (RS):

A. Sl st in each of next 2 dc, ch 3, dc in each dc to next ch-3 sp, (dc, ch 3, dc) in next ch-3 sp, dc in each dc to last dc before next ch-3 sp, sk next dc;

B. ch 3, picot shell in ch-3 sp of next picot shell, ch 3, sk next ch-3 sp and next dc, dc in each dc to next ch-3 sp, (dc, ch 3, dc) in next ch-3 sp, dc in each dc to last dc before next ch-3 sp, sk next dc;

C. ch 3, **half picot shell** (*see Special Stitches*) in next picot shell, ch 7, sk next 2 picot shells, half picot shell in next picot shell;

D. ch 3, sk next ch-3 sp and dc, dc in each dc to next ch-3 sp, (dc, ch 3, dc) in next ch-3 sp, dc in each dc to last dc before next ch-3 sp, sk next dc, *ch 3, picot shell in ch-3 sp of next picot shell, ch 3, sk next ch-3 sp and dc, dc in each dc to next ch-3 sp, (dc, ch 3, dc) in ch-3 sp, dc in

each dc to last dc before next ch-3 sp, sk next dc, rep from * twice more;

E. ch 3, half picot shell in ch-3 sp of next picot shell, ch 7, sk next 2 picot shells, half picot shell in ch-3 sp of next picot shell;

F. ch 3, sk next ch-3 sp and dc, dc in each dc to next ch-3 sp, (dc, ch 3, dc) in next ch-3 sp, dc in each dc to last dc before next ch-3 sp, sk next dc, ch 3, picot shell in ch-3 sp of next picot shell, ch 3, sk next ch-3 sp and dc, dc in each dc to next ch-3 sp, (dc, ch 3, dc) in ch-3 sp, dc in each dc to last dc before next ch-3 sp, sk next dc, ch 3, [dc, ch 3] twice in next ch-3 sp, join in 3rd ch of beg ch-3.

Rnd 2:

A. Sl st in next dc, ch 3, dc in each dc to next ch-3 sp, (2 dc, ch 3, 2 dc) in ch-3 sp, dc in each dc to last dc before next ch-3 sp, sk next dc;

B. ch 3, picot shell in ch-3 sp of next picot shell, ch 3, sk next ch-3 sp and dc, dc in each dc to next ch-3 sp, (2 dc, ch 3, 2 dc) in ch-3 sp, dc in each dc to last dc before next ch-3 sp, sk next dc;

C. ch 3, picot shell in center ch of ch-7 at underarm;

D. ch 3, sk next ch-3 sp and dc, dc in each dc to next ch-3 sp, (2 dc, ch 3, 2 dc) in next ch-3 sp, dc in each dc to last dc before next ch-3 sp, sk next dc, *ch 3, picot shell in ch-3 sp of next picot shell, ch 3, sk next ch-3 sp and dc, dc in each dc to next ch-3 sp, (2 dc, ch 3, 2 dc) in ch-3 sp, dc in each dc to last dc before next ch-3 sp, sk next dc, rep from * twice;

E. ch 3, picot shell in center ch of ch-7 at underarm;

F. ch 3, sk next ch-3 sp and dc, dc in each dc to next ch-3 sp, (dc, ch 3, dc) in ch-3 sp, dc in each dc to last dc before next ch-3 sp, sk next dc, ch 3, picot shell in ch-3 sp of next picot shell, ch 3, sk next ch-3 sp and dc, dc in each dc to next ch-3 sp, (dc, ch 3, dc) in ch-3 sp, dc in each dc to last dc before next ch-3 sp, sk next dc and ch-3 sp, ch 3, picot shell in next ch-3 sp, ch 3, join in 3rd ch of beg ch-3.

Rnd 3: Sl st in next dc, ch 3, dc in each dc to next ch-3 sp, (dc, ch 3, dc) in ch-3 sp, dc in each dc to last dc before next ch-3 sp, sk next dc, *ch 3, picot shell in next picot shell, ch 3, sk next ch-3 sp and dc, dc in each dc to next ch-3 sp, (dc, ch 3, dc) in ch-3 sp, dc in each dc to last dc before next ch-3 sp, sk next dc, rep from * to last picot shell, ch 3, picot shell in last picot shell, ch 3, join in 3rd ch of beg ch-3.

Rnd 4: Sl st in next dc, ch 3, dc in each dc to next ch-3 sp, (2 dc, ch 3, 2 dc) in ch-3 sp, dc in each dc to last dc before next ch-3 sp, sk next dc, *ch 3, picot shell in next picot shell, ch 3, sk next ch-3 sp and dc, dc in each dc to next ch-3 sp, (2 dc, ch 3, 2 dc) in ch-3 sp, dc in each dc to last dc before next ch-3 sp, sk next dc, rep from * to last picot shell, ch 3, picot shell in last picot shell, ch 3, join in 3rd ch of beg ch-3.

Rnds 5–16: [Rep rnds 3 and 4 alternately] 6 times.

Rnd 17: Rep rnd 3.

Rnd 18: Ch 3, **dc dec** (see Stitch Guide) in next 2 dc, picot, [dc dec in next 3 dc, picot] 3 times, *[**3-dc cl**—see Special Stitches, picot] twice in next ch-3 sp, [dc dec in next 3 dc, picot] 4 times, [3-dc cl, picot] 3 times in next picot shell**, [dc dec in next 3 dc, picot] 4 times, rep from * around, ending last rep at **, join in 3rd ch of beg ch-3. Fasten off.

SLEEVES

Rnd 1 (RS): With RS facing, join in center ch of underarm, **beg 3-dc shell** (see Special Stitches) in same st as join, **3-dc shell** (see Special Stitches) around post of next dc (this dc will appear horizontal), [sk next ch-3 sp, 3-dc shell in next ch-3 sp, 3-dc shell in next picot shell] twice, sk next ch-3 sp, 3-dc shell in next ch-3 sp, sk next ch-3 sp, 3-dc shell around post of next dc (this dc will appear horizontal), join in 3rd ch of beg ch-3 of beg 3-dc shell.

Rnd 2: Sl st in each st to ch-3 sp of beg 3-dc shell, (**beg 3-dc cl**—see Special Stitches, picot, 3-dc cl, ch 1) in same sp, (3-dc cl, picot, 3 dc cl, ch 1) in ch-3 sp of each shell around, join in 3rd ch of beg ch-3 of beg 3-dc shell. Fasten off.

Work other Sleeve in same manner.

NECK EDGING

Row 1 (WS): With WS facing, join yarn with sc in first st of neck edge, *ch 3, sk next 2 sts, sc in next st, rep from * around neck edge to last st, turn. Do not work down vertical back opening. (27 sps)

Row 2: Sl st in first ch-3 sp, (beg 3-dc cl, picot, 3-dc cl) in same sp, *ch 1, sk next ch-3 sp, (3-dc cl, picot, 3-dc cl) in next ch-3 sp, rep from * across. Fasten off.

FINISHING

Sew snaps to back opening evenly sp.

Sew ribbon roses to front, aligned vertically along center of Bodice and evenly sp. ∎

Keira
Layette

SKILL LEVEL

EASY

FINISHED SIZES

Instructions are the same for sizes 6–12 months and 12–18 months. Hook size determines size.

FINISHED MEASUREMENTS

SWEATER
Chest: 27 [29] inches
Length: 10¾ [12¼] inches

BONNET
Circumference: 17½ [19] inches
Length: 7¼ [8½] inches

BOOTIES
Sole: 4¾ [5¼] inches

MATERIALS

- Red Heart Baby TLC medium (worsted) weight acrylic yarn (5 oz/ 358 yds/141g per skein):
    2 skeins #5737 powder pink
- Size C/2/2.75mm [D/3/3.25mm] crochet hook or size needed to obtain gauge
- Tapestry needle
- Sewing needle
- 1¾ yds of ¼–½-inch-wide ribbon
- 8 ribbon roses
- Matching sewing thread

GAUGE

Size C hook: 3½ shells = 4 inches

Size D hook: 3¼ shells = 4 inches

PATTERN NOTES

Weave in ends as work progresses.

Chain-3 at beginning of row counts as double crochet unless otherwise stated.

Join with slip stitch as indicated unless otherwise stated.

Chain-4 at beginning of round counts as double crochet and chain-1 unless otherwise stated.

SPECIAL STITCH

Shell: 5 dc in indicated st or sp.

Small shell: 3 dc in indicated st or sp.

SWEATER
YOKE

Row 1 (RS): Ch 71, dc in 5th ch from hook (*4 sk chs counts as a dc and ch-1*), *ch 1, sk next ch, dc in next ch, rep from * across, turn. (*34 ch sps*)

Row 2: Ch 1, sc in first dc, *ch 4, sc in next dc, rep from * across to beg 4 sk chs, ch 4, sk next ch, sc in next ch, turn.

Row 3: **Ch 3** (*see Pattern Notes*), 2 dc in first sc, sc in next ch-4 sp, [ch 4, sc in next ch-4 sp] 8 times, [**shell** (*see Special Stitches*) in **back lp** (*see Stitch Guide*) of next sc, sc in next ch-4 sp] 17 times, [ch 4, sc in next ch-4 sp] 8 times, 3 dc in last sc, turn.

Row 4: Ch 1, sc in first dc, shell in back lp of next sc, sc in next ch-4 sp, [ch 4, sc in next ch-4 sp] 7 times, [shell in back lp of next sc, sc in center st of next shell] 17 times, shell in back lp of next sc, sc in next ch-4 sp, [ch 4, sc in next ch-4 sp] 7 times, shell in next sc, sc in last st, turn.

Row 5: Ch 3, 2 dc in first sc, sc in center st of next shell, shell in back lp of next sc, sc in next ch-4 sp, [ch 4, sc in next ch-4 sp] 6 times, [shell in back lp of next sc, sc in center st of next shell] 18 times, shell in back lp of next sc, sc in next ch-4 sp, [ch 4, sc in next ch-4 sp] 6 times, shell in back lp of next sc, sc in center st of next shell, 3 dc in last sc, turn.

Row 6: Ch 1, sc in first dc, shell in back lp of next sc, sc in center st of next shell, shell in back lp of next sc, sc in next ch-4 sp, [ch 4, sc in next ch-4 sp] 5 times, [shell in back lp of next sc, sc in center st of next shell] 19 times, shell in back lp of next sc, sc in next ch-4 sp, [ch 4, sc in next ch-4 sp] 5 times, shell in back lp of next sc, sc in center st of next shell, shell in back lp of next sc, sc in last st, turn.

Row 7: Ch 3, 2 dc in first sc, [sc in center st of next shell, shell in back lp of next sc] twice, sc in next ch-4 sp, [ch 4, sc in next ch-4 sp] 4 times, [shell in back lp of next sc, sc in center st of next shell] 20 times, shell in back lp of next sc, sc in next ch-4 sp, [ch 4, sc in next ch-4 sp] 4 times, [shell in back lp of next sc, sc in center st of next shell] twice, 3 dc in last sc, turn.

Row 8: Ch 1, sc in first dc, [shell in back lp of next sc, sc in center st of next shell] twice, shell in back lp of next sc, sc in next ch-4 sp, [ch 4, sc in next ch-4 sp] 3 times, [shell in back lp of next sc, sc in center st of next shell] 21 times, shell in back lp of next sc, sc in next ch-4 sp, [ch 4, sc in next ch-4 sp] twice, shell in back lp of next sc, [sc in center st of next shell, shell in back lp of next sc] twice, sc in last st, turn.

Row 9: Ch 3, 2 dc in first sc, [sc in center st of next shell, shell in back lp of next sc] 3 times, sc in next ch-4 sp, [ch 4, sc in next ch-4 sp] twice, [shell in back lp of next sc, sc in center st of next shell] 22 times, shell in back lp of next sc, sc in next ch-4 sp, [ch 4, sc in next ch-4 sp] twice, [shell in back lp of next sc, sc in center st of next shell] 3 times, 3 dc in last sc, turn.

Row 10: Ch 1, sc in first dc, [shell in back lp of next sc, sc in center st of next shell] 3 times, shell in back lp of next sc, sc in next ch-4 sp, ch 4, sc in next ch-4 sp, [shell in back lp of next sc, sc in center st of next shell] 23 times, shell in back lp of next sc, sc in next ch-4 sp, ch 4, sc in next ch-4 sp, shell in back lp of next sc, [sc in center st of next shell, shell in back lp of next sc] 3 times, sc in last st, turn.

Row 11: Ch 3, 2 dc in first sc, [sc in center st of next shell, shell in back lp of next sc] 4 times, (sc, dc, sc) in next ch-4 sp, [shell in back lp of next sc, sc in center st of next shell] 24 times, shell in back lp of next sc, (sc, dc, sc) in next ch-4 sp, [shell in back lp of next sc, sc in center st of next shell] 4 times, 3 dc in last sc, turn.

Row 12: Ch 1, sc in first dc, [shell in back lp of next sc, sc in center st of next shell] 4 times, shell in back lp of next sc, sc in next dc, [shell in back lp of next sc, sc in center st of next shell] 25 times, shell in back lp of next sc, sc in next dc, [shell in back lp of next sc, sc in center st of next shell] 4 times, shell in back lp of next sc, sc in last st, turn. *(36 shells)*

Row 13: Ch 3, 2 dc in first sc, sc in center st of next shell, *shell in back lp of next sc, sc in center st of next shell, rep from * to last sc, 3 dc in last sc, turn. *(35 shells)*

BODY

Row 1 (WS): Ch 1, sc in first dc, [shell in back lp of next sc, sc in center st of next shell] 5 times, ch 3, sk next 7 shells, sc in center st of next shell, [shell in back lp of next sc, sc in center st of next shell] 10 times, ch 3, sk next 7 shells, sc in center st of next shell, [shell in back lp of next sc, sc in center st of next shell] 5 times, sc in last st, turn. *(20 shells)*

Row 2: Ch 3, 2 dc in first sc, sc in center st of next shell, [shell in back lp of next sc, sc in center st of next shell] 4 times, shell in back lp of next sc, (sc, dc, sc) in next ch-3 sp, [shell in back lp of next sc, sc in center st of next shell] 10 times, shell in back lp of next sc, (sc, dc, sc) in next ch-3 sp, [shell in back lp of next sc, sc in center st of next shell] 5 times, 3 dc in last sc, turn. *(21 shells)*

Row 3: Ch 1, sc in first dc, [shell in back lp of next sc, sc in center st of next shell] 5 times, shell in back lp of next sc, sc in next dc, [shell in back lp of next sc, sc in center st of next shell] 11 times, shell in back lp of next sc, sc in next dc, [shell in back lp of next sc, sc in center st of next shell] 5 times, shell in back lp of next sc, sc in last st, turn. *(24 shells)*

Row 4: Ch 3, 2 dc in first sc, sc in center st of next shell, *shell in back lp of next sc, sc in center st of next shell, rep from * across to last sc, 3 dc in last sc, turn. *(23 shells)*

Row 5: Ch 1, sc in first dc, *shell in back lp of next sc, sc in center st of next shell, rep from * across, working last sc in last st, turn.

Rows 6–13 [6–15]: [Rep rows 4 and 5 alternately] 4 [5] times.

Row 14 [16]: Rep row 4.

FRONT & NECK TRIM
With RS facing, sc in each sc and 2 sc in each dc across right front edge, 4 sc in neck corner, 2 sc in each sp across neck edge, 4 sc in next neck corner, sc in each sc and 2 sc in each dc across left front edge. Fasten off.

SLEEVES
Rnd 1 (WS): With WS facing and leaving long tail, **join** *(see Pattern Notes)* yarn in center ch of 1 underarm, *shell in back lp of next sc, sc in center st of next shell, rep from * across to last sc, shell in back lp of last sc, sc in same ch as joining sl st, sl st in each of next 3 sts, turn. *(8 shells)*

Rnds 2 & 3: *Shell in back lp of next sc, sc in center st of next shell, rep from * around to last sc, shell in back lp of last sc, sc in same st as last sl st of previous rnd, sl st in each of next 3 sts, turn.

Note: For longer sleeves, rep rnds 2 and 3 to desired length, ending with a WS rnd.

CUFF
Rnd 1 (RS): Ch 1, sc in same st as last sl st of previous rnd, sc in next st, [sk next 3 sts, sc in each of next 3 sts] 7 times, sk next 3 sts, sc in next st, join in first sc.

Rnds 2 & 3: Ch 1, sc in each sc around, join in first sc.

Work Sleeve in rem armhole.

FINISHING
With long tails, tack sps at underarms together.

Sew 3 ribbon roses evenly sp on right front edge.

BONNET
Rnd 1 (RS): Ch 6, **join** *(see Pattern Notes)* in first ch to form ring, **ch 3** *(see Pattern Notes)*, 19 dc in ring, join in 3rd ch of beg ch-3. *(20 dc)*

Rnd 2: **Ch 4** *(see Pattern Notes)*, *dc in next dc, ch 1, rep from * around, join in 3rd of beg ch-4.

Rnd 3: Ch 1, sc in same ch as beg ch-1, ch 5, *sc in next dc, ch 5, rep from * around, join in first sc. *(20 ch sps)*

Rnd 4: Sl st in each of next 3 chs of next ch-5 sp, ch 1, sc in same ch as beg ch-1, *shell *(see Special Stitches)* in **back lp** *(see Stitch Guide)* of next sc, [sc in next ch-5 sp, ch 4] 4 times**, sc in next ch-5 sp, rep from * around, ending last rep at **, join in first sc, sl st in each of next 3 sts, turn. *(4 shells, 16 ch sps)*

Rnd 5: Ch 1, sc in same ch beg ch-1, *shell in **back lp** (see Stitch Guide) of next sc, [sc in next ch-4 sp, ch 4] 3 times, sc in next ch-4 sp, shell in back lp of next sc**, sc in center st of next shell, rep from * around, ending last rep at **, join in first sc, sl st in each of next 3 sts, turn. (8 shells, 12 ch sps)

Rnd 6: Ch 1, sc in same ch as last sl st of previous rnd, *shell in back lp of next st, sc in center st of next shell, shell in back lp of next sc, [sc in next ch-4 sp, ch 4] twice, sc in next ch-4 sp, shell in back lp of next sc**, sc in center st of next shell, rep from * around, ending last rep at **, join in first sc, sl st in each of next 3 sts, turn. (12 shells, 8 ch sps)

Rnd 7: Ch 1, sc in same ch as beg ch 1, *shell in back lp of next sc, sc in center st of next shell, shell in back lp of next sc, sc in next ch-4 sp, ch 4, sc in next ch-4 sp, shell in back lp of next sc, sc in center st of next shell, shell in back lp of next sc**, sc in center st of next shell, rep from * around, ending last rep at **, join in first sc, sl st in each of next 3 sts, turn. (16 shells, 4 ch sps)

Rnd 8: Ch 1, sc in same ch as beg ch-1, [shell in back lp of next sc, sc in center st of next shell] twice, shell in back lp of next sc, sc in next ch-4 sp, *[shell in back lp of next sc, sc in center st of next shell] 4 times, shell in back lp of next sc, sc in next ch-4 sp, rep from * twice, shell in back lp of next sc, sc in center st of next shell, shell in back lp of next sc, join in first sc, sl st in each of next 3 sts, turn. (20 shells)

Row 9 (RS): Now working in rows, ch 1, sc in same ch as beg ch-1, [shell in back lp of next sc, sc in center st of next shell] 15 times. Leaving rem sts unworked, turn. (15 shells)

Row 10: Ch 3, 2 dc in first sc, sc in center st of next shell, *shell in back lp of next sc, sc in center st of next shell, rep from * across to last sc, 3 dc in last sc, turn. (14 shells)

Row 11: Ch 1, sc in first dc, *shell in back lp of next sc, sc in center st of next shell, rep from * across, working last sc in last st, turn. (15 shells)

Rows 12–17 [12–19]: [Rep rows 10 and 11 alternately] 3 [4] times.

Row 18 [20]: Rep row 10.

FRONT EDGING
Row 1 (WS): Ch 1, sc in first dc, *ch 5, sc in next sc, ch 5, sc in center st of next shell, rep from * across, working last sc last st, turn. (30 ch sps)

Row 2: Sk first sc, sl st in each of next 3 chs, ch 1, sc in same ch as beg ch-1, shell in back lp of next sc, sc in next ch-5 sp, [ch 5, sc in next ch-5 sp, shell in back lp of next sc, sc in next ch-5 sp] 14 times, turn.

Row 3: Sl st in first sc, sl st in each of next 3 dc, *shell in back lp of next sc, sc in next 5-ch sp, shell in back lp of next sc, sc in center st of next shell, rep from * across, turn. (28 shells)

Row 4: Sl st in first sc, sl st in each of next 3 dc, *shell in back lp of next sc, sc in center st of next shell, rep from * across. Do not turn. (27 shells)

NECK EDGING
Row 1 (RS): Working across side of Bonnet, work 12 [15] sc evenly sp across edge, working across back neck edge, work 9 sc evenly sp, working across next side of Bonnet, work 12 [15] sc evenly sp across. Leaving rem sts unworked, turn.

Rows 2 & 3: Ch 1, sc in each sc across, turn. At end of last row, fasten off.

FINISHING
Cut a 30 [32]-inch length of ribbon. Weave ribbon through row 1 of Front Edging for ties.

Sew 3 ribbon roses to center back of Bonnet.

BOOTIE
MAKE 2.
SOLE & FOOT
Rnd 1 (RS): Ch 17, dc in 3rd ch from hook, 2 dc in next ch, dc in each of next 12 chs, 5 dc in last ch, working in unused lps on opposite of foundation ch, dc in each of next 12 chs, 2 dc in last ch, **join** (see Pattern Notes) in 2nd ch of beg 2 sk chs. (34 dc)

Rnd 2: Ch 2, 2 hdc in each of next 3 sts, hdc in each of next 11 sts, 2 hdc in each of next 6 sts, hdc in each of next 11 sts, 2 hdc in each of last 3 sts, join in 2nd ch of beg ch-2. *(46 hdc)*

Rnd 3: Ch 2, [2 hdc in next st, hdc in next st] 3 times, hdc in each of next 11 sts, [2 hdc in next st, hdc in next st] 6 times, hdc in each of next 11 sts, [2 hdc in next st, hdc in next st] 3 times, join in 2nd ch of beg ch-2. *(58 hdc)*

Rnd 4: Ch 1, **bpsc** *(see Stitch Guide)* around each hdc, join in beg ch-1, turn.

Rnds 5–10: Ch 1, sc in **back lp** *(see Stitch Guide)* of each sc around, join in beg ch-1, turn. At end of last rnd, fasten off.

INSTEP

Row 1 (RS): With RS facing, count 25 sts from joining of last rnd, join yarn with sc in same st, sc in each of next 9 sts, sk next st, sl st in next st on side of foot, turn.

Rows 2–11: Ch 1, sc in each of first 10 sc, sk next st, sl st in next st on side of foot, turn. At end of last row, do not turn.

CUFF

Rnd 1 (RS): **Ch 4** *(see Pattern Notes)*, sk next st, *dc in next st, ch 1, sk next st, rep from * around, join in 3rd ch of beg ch-4. Do not turn. *(20 ch sps)*

Rnd 2: Ch 1, sc in same ch as beg ch-1, [ch 5, sk next dc, sc in next dc] 9 times, ch 2, join with dc in first sc, turn. *(10 sps)*

Rnd 3: Ch 1, sc in sp formed by joining dc, *small shell* *(see Special Stitches)* in back lp of next sc, sc in next ch-5 sp, rep from * across to last sc, small shell in last sc, join in first sc, sl st in each of next 2 sts, turn.

Rnds 4–6: Ch 1, sc in same st as beg ch-1, *small shell in back lp of next sc, sc in center st of next small shell, rep from * across to last sc, small shell in back lp of last sc, join in first sc, sl st in each of next 2 sts, turn.

Rnd 7: Ch 1, sc in same ch as beg ch-1, *small shell in back lp of next sc, sc in center st of next small shell, rep from * across to last sc, small shell in back lp of last sc, join in first sc. Fasten off.

FINISHING

Cut 2 (12-inch) lengths of ribbon. Weave ribbon through rnd 1 of each Cuff and tie in a bow.

Sew 1 ribbon rose to instep of each Bootie. ∎

Annie's® *Beautiful Baby Boutique II* is published by Annie's, 306 East Parr Road, Berne, IN 46711. Printed in USA. Copyright © 2013, 2017 Annie's. All rights reserved. This publication may not be reproduced in part or in whole without written permission from the publisher.

RETAIL STORES: If you would like to carry this pattern book or any other Annie's publication, visit AnniesWSL.com

Every effort has been made to ensure that the instructions in this pattern book are complete and accurate. We cannot, however, take responsibility for human error, typographical mistakes or variations in individual work. Please visit AnniesCustomerService.com to check for pattern updates.

ISBN: 978-1-59635-851-5

STITCH GUIDE

STITCH ABBREVIATIONS

beg	begin/begins/beginning
bpdc	back post double crochet
bpsc	back post single crochet
bptr	back post treble crochet
CC	contrasting color
ch(s)	chain(s)
ch-	refers to chain or space previously made (i.e., ch-1 space)
ch sp(s)	chain space(s)
cl(s)	cluster(s)
cm	centimeter(s)
dc	double crochet (singular/plural)
dc dec	double crochet 2 or more stitches together, as indicated
dec	decrease/decreases/decreasing
dtr	double treble crochet
ext	extended
fpdc	front post double crochet
fpsc	front post single crochet
fptr	front post treble crochet
g	gram(s)
hdc	half double crochet
hdc dec	half double crochet 2 or more stitches together, as indicated
inc	increase/increases/increasing
lp(s)	loop(s)
MC	main color
mm	millimeter(s)
oz	ounce(s)
pc	popcorn(s)
rem	remain/remains/remaining
rep(s)	repeat(s)
rnd(s)	round(s)
RS	right side
sc	single crochet (singular/plural)
sc dec	single crochet 2 or more stitches together, as indicated
sk	skip/skipped/skipping
sl st(s)	slip stitch(es)
sp(s)	space(s)/spaced
st(s)	stitch(es)
tog	together
tr	treble crochet
trtr	triple treble
WS	wrong side
yd(s)	yard(s)
yo	yarn over

YARN CONVERSION

OUNCES TO GRAMS		GRAMS TO OUNCES	
1	28.4	25	⅞
2	56.7	40	1⅔
3	85.0	50	1¾
4	113.4	100	3½

UNITED STATES		UNITED KINGDOM
sl st (slip stitch)	=	sc (single crochet)
sc (single crochet)	=	dc (double crochet)
hdc (half double crochet)	=	htr (half treble crochet)
dc (double crochet)	=	tr (treble crochet)
tr (treble crochet)	=	dtr (double treble crochet)
dtr (double treble crochet)	=	ttr (triple treble crochet)
skip	=	miss

Single crochet decrease (sc dec):
(Insert hook, yo, draw lp through) in each of the sts indicated, yo, draw through all lps on hook.

Example of 2-sc dec

Half double crochet decrease (hdc dec):
(Yo, insert hook, yo, draw lp through) in each of the sts indicated, yo, draw through all lps on hook.

Example of 2-hdc dec

Reverse single crochet (reverse sc):
Ch 1, sk first st, working from left to right, insert hook in next st from front to back, draw up lp on hook, yo and draw through both lps on hook.

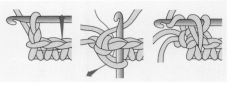

Chain (ch):
Yo, pull through lp on hook.

Single crochet (sc):
Insert hook in st, yo, pull through st, yo, pull through both lps on hook.

Double crochet (dc):
Yo, insert hook in st, yo, pull through st, [yo, pull through 2 lps] twice.

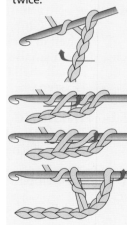

Double crochet decrease (dc dec):
(Yo, insert hook, yo, draw lp through, yo, draw through 2 lps on hook) in each of the sts indicated, yo, draw through all lps on hook.

Example of 2-dc dec

Front loop (front lp) Back loop (back lp)

Front Loop   Back Loop

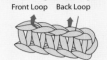

Front post stitch (fp): Back post stitch (bp):
When working post st, insert hook from right to left around post of st on previous row.

Back   Front

Post of Stitch

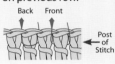

Half double crochet (hdc):
Yo, insert hook in st, yo, pull through st, yo, pull through all 3 lps on hook.

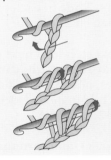

Double treble crochet (dtr):
Yo 3 times, insert hook in st, yo, pull through st, [yo, pull through 2 lps] 4 times.

Treble crochet decrease (tr dec):
Holding back last lp of each st, tr in each of the sts indicated, yo, pull through all lps on hook.

Example of 2-tr dec

Slip stitch (sl st):
Insert hook in st, pull through both lps on hook.

Chain color change (ch color change)
Yo with new color, draw through last lp on hook.

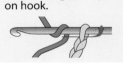

Double crochet color change (dc color change)
Drop first color, yo with new color, draw through last 2 lps of st.

Treble crochet (tr):
Yo twice, insert hook in st, yo, pull through st, [yo, pull through 2 lps] 3 times.

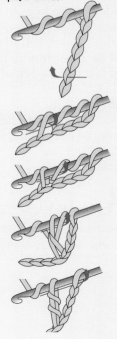